THE ORGANIC CANNER

A Guide to Preserving Real Food

By: Daisy Luther

Illustrated by C. Morgan

Table of Contents

Introduction

Disclaimer:

Due to the fact that we live in a litigious society, a disclaimer is necessary in a book of this type.

The information in this book outlines the principles of safe home canning and uses the most recent recommendations that were available at the time of publication.

Ultimately, though, you bear the responsibility for your own food safety practices. By reading this book, you consent to be responsible for your decisions to use this material. You specifically acknowledge that the author assumes no liability to you or any third party for any direct, indirect, incident, special, punitive, or consequential damages for personal injury or wrongful death arising from any action taken by you or others upon reliance of the information in this book.

Introduction

From time immemorial, preserving the harvest was a vital preparation to face the barren winter months ahead. Different methods have been used throughout the ages and many of them, although modernized somewhat, are still used today.

One of my favorite methods of preservation is canning. Canning is the perfect solution for those seeking natural food sources, for gardeners, for those seeking a more self-reliant life, and for those interested in preparedness.

Once you have a pressure canner (and you conquer the fear of blowing yourself up with it!) you can preserve nearly anything. By creating meals right in the jars, you can provide your family with instant tasty nutrition.

For a year, we lived in an area with an occasionally shaky grasp on electricity. We were able to test out our preps several times when living there and our home canned meals turned out to be one of the best time investments that I have made.

During a power outage situation, a hot meal can be as simple as opening a jar, pouring the contents into a pot, and placing it on the woodstove for about half an hour.

I love to go into the pantry and look at my shelves full of gleaming jars, full of meat, fruits, and vegetables that I either grew myself or carefully selected. My favorite canned item of all has to be "meals". We have shelves full of soups, stews, and other entrees.

These items are very simple to prepare. If you use garden produce when possible and combine it with ingredients purchased on sale, you can have many "instant" meals prepared at a very affordable price – and the best part is, you know exactly what's in it!!!!

Another valuable benefit to canning is that you are not reliant on the electrical system for your food – if the power goes out, you won't have these items rotting in your freezer. They will be sitting there on a shelf, awaiting your mealtime. In an absolute worst case scenario, since all foods are thoroughly cooked by the pressure canning process, you could eat them at room temperature, right out of the jar.

Thank you for reading and I wish you happy canning!

The
 Organic Canning 
Manifesto

A lot of people look at my canning projects and they shake their heads. "Why would you work that hard when you can just go to the grocery store?"

The list of reasons is long and distinguished.

Most of all, I want our food to actually be food.

I don't want to serve food-like substances, concocted in a factory after being created by chemists who throw around words like "mouthfeel" and "sodium ethyl parahydroxybenzoate". I don't want to eat something that was chemically created to taste like another item, but offered in the altered form because it gives a higher profit margin to Kraft or Kellogg's.

I don't want to serve genetically mutated organisms that were begun in a petri dish at the labs of Monsanto. A vast percentage of the foods at the grocery store, even those in the produce aisle, are the end result of a genetically sterilized seed that was also altered to contain pesticides and mutations that allow it to grow bigger, faster, and more brightly colored. GMO foods were not thoroughly tested before being rushed to the market by Monsanto in their desire to create a world food monopoly. In independent studies, laboratory animals that are fed a GMO diet, develop multiple organ failure, sterility, greater allergic responses, high rates of offspring mortality and premature death.

I don't want to serve items processed from the genetically modified corn and soy that infects more than 80% of the food in the grocery store. With factors like cross-contamination and the food chain itself, almost 100% of grocery store foods are tainted with genetic modifications.

I can't afford to hit the health food store for every bite we put in our mouths. This is the source that comes to mind for most people when they think about "organic" or "natural" foods. But for most of us this is financially out of reach. I can save money by getting locally grown foods when they are in season, cleaning them carefully, and preserving them myself for the winter ahead. This allows room in my budget for weekly grocery items like organic hormone-free milk.

Eating seasonally provides nutritional benefits. I grow as much organic produce as I can on my small lot. I supplement what I grow with produce from a couple of local farms, where I have been lucky enough to forge a relationship with the farmers. Our food does not come from thousands of miles away, picked while green and left to ripen in a box. It is picked and home-processed at the peak of its freshness as often as possible, conserving as many nutrients as we can for the winter ahead.

I refuse to consume the growth hormones, antibiotics and other medications that are given to factory farmed meat animals. I spend a little bit more money and buy our meats in bulk from a local Mennonite butcher shop or a farmer that I know personally. They do not use any chemicals in the farming of their animals and the livestock is fed what livestock naturally eats – grass, hay, bugs and seeds. Furthermore, the animals are farmed humanely, reducing hormones like cortisol that are released when any animal (two-legged or four-legged) is under stress.

Home-canned food is the fastest "fast food" around. By preserving entire meals in jars, I can get a healthy and delicious meal on the table in a fraction of the time it would take to take the truck to a McDonald's drive-thru and get the food home. Quite literally, a pot of homemade soup is steaming in a bowl in less than 5 minutes.

The hands-on work that I put in to cooking our food for the rest of the year during the growing season is probably less hands-on time than I would take producing the same meals throughout the year, one meal at a time. The reason for this is that I produce 8-16 meals at a time – perhaps 2 hours of preparation time and 2 hours of processing time when I am doing other things. That is an average 20 minutes per meal, with half of that time NOT being spent in the kitchen – that time is spent just waiting for the processing time to be over.

This choice might not be for everyone. It might not be for every meal. If you don't have a lot of interest in where your food comes from or what it contains, then it is probably not the option for you. But as someone who firmly believes that our nutritional choices are the basis for our overall long-term physical and mental health, as the parent of a child with allergies and chemical sensitivities, and as an activist who refuses to support the food monopoly and toxic practices of companies like Monsanto and Dow Chemical, this is the choice for me.

❧ Canning 101 ❧

First, if you've never canned before, you need to know the basics. When you purchase your canning gear, be sure to thoroughly read the instructions. If your instruction manual disagrees with anything I say here, the instruction manual wins, as these are general instructions based on my own equipment.

The recipes in the book will tell you whether the food should be water bath canned or pressure canned. Water bath canning is only for high-acid foods like fruits and pickles. For everything else, you should use a pressure canner.

A note about sanitizing: some folks get really stressed out about this. I'm providing the best practices for you, but please keep in mind that you are not performing open heart surgery. Nearly all canning recipes have to be processed for more than 10 minutes, which, in conjunction with the pre-sterilization you have performed, should keep your food safe and healthy.

Jar Prep

Your preserved food is only as sanitary as the vessels you put it into. An important step that must not be overlooked is sanitizing and preparing the jars, lids, and rings. There are several methods for this.

The Dishwasher Method

If you have a dishwasher, this is easy. Just run it on the sanitizing cycle right before you begin canning. The dishwasher will keep the jars hot until you are ready to fill them. The heat from the dishwasher will also make the rubber on the jar flat more pliable and ready to seal.

The Water Bath Canner Method

Assuming that your jars are clean and all you need to do is sterilize them, you can use your water bath canner for this. Place the jars in the canner, on the rack. Pour in enough water that it goes over the opening of the jars and fills them. Bring the canner to a boil and allow it to boil for 10 minutes. Then use your jar lifter and remove the jars, placing them upside down on a towel or drying rack to drain.
Timesaving Hint: Reuse the hot water for canning once the jars are filled and lidded.

The Oven Method

You can also use your oven to sterilize your jars. Preheat your oven to 225 degrees Fahrenheit. Place your jars in a roasting pan and slide them into the oven for at least 20 minutes. At that point, you can turn off the heat, but leave the jars in there until they are ready to be packed.
Warning: (this is kind of a "duh" but I'll say it anyway!) The jars will be hotter than heck when you take them out of the oven – take care not to burn yourself when filling them and placing them in the canner!

Sanitizing the Lids

It wouldn't do to put all that effort into making sure your jars are clean and then top them off with un-sanitized lids!
In a small saucepan, bring to a simmer enough water to cover your flats and rings. Do not bring the flats to a rolling boil, as this could damage the sealing compound. Keep the lids in the hot water and remove them with sterilized tongs or a lid lifter (a cool little magnetic wand) when you are ready to put them on the jars.

Breathe...

Water Bath Canning

Water bath canning is a safe method for preserving high-acid foods. Some examples of foods that can be canned in a water bath are:

- Jams and jellies
- Fruit
- Applesauce
- Pickles
- Tomato products

For water bath canning you must have the following tools:

- Big canning pot
- Rack (if you don't have a rack you can use a folded towel in the bottom of the pot)
- Jar lifter
- Jar funnel
- Jars

These items are the minimum tools you need for canning properly and safely. There are all sorts of other gadgets out there, like items that help you measure headspace and lid lifters with a little magnet on the end, but if you have the above items – you are ready to can!

Then, of course, you need:

- Jars
- Flats (also called snap lids)
- Rings

Step-by-Step

Okay....your product is on the stove, bubbling merrily away......

Sanitize your jars, lids, and rings. If you have a dishwasher, you can wash them in the dishwasher – the heat from it is enough to sterilize everything. Otherwise, you need to boil the items for at least 10 minutes, lifting them carefully in and out with the jar lifter. Leave the items in the dishwasher or the hot water until ready to use. Another option is to add 10 minutes to your processing time in the water bath but this can affect the quality of your product. I'm notoriously lazy and use the dishwasher.

Prepare your canner. Place your rack in the bottom of your canner and fill your canner with water, leaving about 3-5 inches at the top to allow for room for your filled jars. If you don't have a rack, you can line the bottom with a folded towel. Bring your water to a boil. Because it takes forever and a day to bring that much water to a boil, I generally start it while I am prepping my food.

Fill your jars. Line up your jars on a heat proof surface near the stove. You can place a towel on the counter to protect it from the hot, filled jars. Using the funnel, ladle the prepared product into the jars, leaving the headspace recommended in your recipe.

Put on your lids. With a dry clean dishtowel, carefully wipe the lip of the filled jars, removing any residue. Place the flats on each jar, then finger tighten the rings – you don't have to really torque on them - the job of the rings it to hold the flats in place until they seal.

Place your jars in the canner. With your handy-dandy jar lifter, place the closed jars carefully into the canner. Put them in gently because, as you know, boiling water **hurts** when it splashes on you. Be careful not to let the jars touch because they could break when they bump together in the boiling water. Make sure the lids are all completely submerged under the water. They don't have to be under by inches - just covered.

Process the jars. Put the lid back on and return the canner back to a rolling boil. Don't start clocking your processing time until the water is at a full boil. Then just leave the jars in the water bath for the amount of time required in your recipe. If you want to sound productive you can refer to this as "processing your jars".

Remove the jars from the canner. Using your jar lifter, carefully remove the jars from the boiling water. Tip the jars to the side to allow the hot water to drip off the top. Then place the jar on your towel or heat proof surface.

Now, leave 'em alone! Allow 12-24 hours for the jars to cool and seal. You will hear a musical "pop" "plink" "ping" noise as the jars seal in the cool air – that is the lid getting sucked down and forming a seal to the lip of the jar.

When you are ready to store the jars, you can remove the rings. This keeps your rings from rusting because of moisture trapped between the metal ring and the jar. Test the seal by pushing down with your finger. If it pops back and forth it is not sealed. Put it in the refrigerator and use the unsealed product in the next few weeks. Store your sealed little gems in a cool, dark place. (It's okay to peek in and admire them from time to time.)

Pressure Canning

Low-acid foods have to be preserved at a higher temperature than high-acid foods. The low-acid environment welcomes the growth of bacteria like botulism, a form of food poisoning that can cause permanent nerve damage or even death.

Pressure canning exceeds the temperature of water bath canning, getting your product into the safety zone. The temperature must reach 240 degrees Fahrenheit, which can only be achieved through steam under pressure.

All vegetables (except for tomatoes which are botanically a fruit), meats, seafood, and poultry must be preserved in a pressure canner.

I'll be honest – I was utterly terrified the first time I used my pressure canner – I was certain I was going to blow up my kitchen. Back this up with the mental image of me screaming and dropping the regulator (that little black round thing you see on the top) when I put it on askew and the canner began to make a gosh-awful whistling noise.

But after successfully p-canning a couple of times, I'm actually equally as comfortable using this method as I am using the water bath method. There are some recipes that can use either canner, and when it's an option I nearly always choose the pressure canner because it is far faster for those recipes.

Pep-talk is over – let's p-can!!!!

For pressure canning you need:

- Jars
- Flats (also called snap lids)
- Rings
- Pressure canner with valves, seals and gauges
- Rack (if you don't have a rack you can use a folded towel in the bottom of the pot)
- Jar lifter

- Jar funnel

Like water bath canning, you can get all the gadgets if you want too, but these are the essentials.

Instructions in this book are for a dial gauge canner. If you happen to have a weighted gauge canner, your available weights for canning are 5, 10, and 15 pounds. If the pressure required to can a certain food is not one of these numbers, go up to the next highest pressure. For example, i the recipe calls for 11 PSI, then use the 15 pound weight setting.

Step-by-Step

One thing you will notice about pressure canning is that nearly all of the steps are identical to the method for water bath canning. Differences (in italics) are really only related to the equipment. So, once you have learned to use your pressure canner correctly, you will find it every bit as easy as water bath canning.

Sanitize your jars, lids, and rings. If you have a dishwasher, you can wash them in the dishwasher – the heat from it is enough to sterilize everything. Otherwise, you need to boil them for at least 10 minutes, lifting them carefully in and out with the jar lifter. Leave the items in the dishwasher or the hot water until ready to use.

Prepare your canner. *Place your rack or folded towel in the bottom of your canner add about 3 inches of water to the canner. Most p-canners have a line to which you fill the water. In pressure canning it is not necessary for the water to cover the lids. (Always check the instructions on your individual canner – it there is a discrepancy, go with the instructions that came with your product.) At this point, you can turn the burner on low to begin warming the water, but don't bring it to a boil yet.*

Fill your jars. Line up your jars on the counter near the stove. If the surface is not heat proof, place a towel on the counter first because the filled jars will be very hot. Using the funnel, ladle the prepared product into the jars, leaving the headspace recommended in your recipe.

Put on your lids. With a dry clean dishtowel, carefully wipe the lip of the filled jars, making sure to get any residue of food off. Place the flats on each jar, then finger tighten the rings – you don't have to really torque on them.

Place your jars in the canner. *Place the closed jars into the canner. Be careful not to let the jars touch because not only could they could break when they bump together in the boiling water, but in p-canning the steam must be able to completely circulate around the jars.*

Build steam in the canner. *Before putting the lid on the canner, check the vent pipe every single time to be sure it is clear. Place the lid firmly on the canner, latching it as per the specifics of your canner, and increase the* heat to bring the water to a boil. At this point steam should be coming out the vent pipe. Reduce the heat until a moderate amount of steam is coming steadily out the pipe for 10 minutes. The purpose of this is to release the air and build up the steam inside the canner. If you don't give it the whole 10 minutes, your canner will not build pressure. As patience is not my strong point, I learned this from experience.

Close the vent. After exhausting the steam for 10 minutes, depending on your canner, either close the petcock or place the weighted regulator on the vent pipe. When I place the regulator on, I always put a dishtowel around my hand, because, yeah, steam is HOT. It sometimes makes a loud high-pitched noise when you are putting the regulator on - I scared myself the first time and screamed, causing my child to think I'd gone and blown myself up. (Teehee.) Don't be alarmed by the various rattling, whistling, and bubbling noises. P-canning is loud business.

Pressurize the canner. Turn up the heat on the burner and wait until the gauge has reached the desired pressure. (Pressure will differ based on altitudes and recipes). This usually takes 3-5 minutes. Note: if you lose pressure during processing you must re-start the processing time. Adjust the heat to maintain the pressure – this takes practice. Monitor your canner throughout the processing time to be sure the pressure is maintained. I have found that approximately #4 on the dial on my electric stove keeps my pressure between 10-12 pounds quite steadily.

Release the pressure. When your processing time is over it is time to release the pressure. It couldn't be easier. Turn off the burner. Take the canner off the burner and put it on a heat-proof surface. Walk away. Allow the canner to return to room temperature and release pressure naturally. Don't try to do anything to cool it down faster - that is how people get hurt p-canning. Pressure is completely reduced when the air vent/cover lock and overpressure plug have dropped and no steam escapes when the pressure regulator is tilted. The gauge, if your canner has one, should be completely at zero. This can take 45 minutes to an hour and cannot be rushed!

Open the vent. When pressure is gone, open the petcock, or remove the weighted regulator. If the regulator doesn't want to come off - there is likely still some pressure in the canner. Don't force it - walk away for another 15 minutes. Once the vent is open, leave the canner for another 2-5 minutes.

Remove the jars from the canner. *Use potholders to protect your hands while you unlatch the lid of your p-canner. Very carefully remove the lid to the canner, facing it away from you so that you are not burned by the steam that will rush out.* Using your jar lifter, carefully remove the jars from the canner, one by one. Then place the jar on your towel or heat-proof surface.

Allow 12-24 hours for the jars to cool and seal. Let the jars stand in a draft-free place without being moved or bumped, usually overnight. Jars that are sealed properly will bubble away on the counter for quite some time after they are removed from the p-canner. You will hear a musical "pop" as the jars seal in the cool air – that is the lid getting sucked down and forming a seal on the jar. When you are ready to store the jars, you can remove the rings and then test the seal by pushing down with your finger. If it pops back and forth it is not sealed. Put it in the refrigerator and use the unsealed product right away. Store your sealed jars in a cool, dark place.

Altitude Adjustment

My canning friends, sometimes we have to look at our situations and say to ourselves, "I need an altitude adjustment."

It's all science, like so much of canning is.

At sea level, and up to 1000 feet above sea level, water boils at 212 degrees Fahrenheit.

However, once you get above the 1000 foot mark, the changes in atmospheric pressure means that your boiling point is actually LOWER than 212F.

Altitude	Temperature at which Water Boils
10,000	194°F
8,000	197°F
6,000	201°F
4,000	204°F
2,000	208°F
0 (Sea Level)	212°F

Because of these differences in the boiling point, we must add extra processing time in order to make our food safe. It simply isn't worth the risk to cut out a few minutes of canning time, so learn your altitude and adjust your times accordingly.

I had to re-calculate all of the times and pressures that I had been using when I moved from sea level here to the mountains at 3000 feet.

Water Bath Canning Adjustments

For water bath canning, food safety requirements mean that the goodies inside your jars should reach 212F, and if it doesn't you have to add to your processing time in order to make your preserved food safe.

For water bath canning, add 2 minutes of processing time for each 1000 feet about 1000 feet that you are.

To use the following chart, take the processing time and add to it based on your elevation.

Adjustments for Water Bath Canning	
Elevation	+ time
1000-2999	5 minutes
3000-5999	10 minutes
6000-7999	15 minutes
8000-10,000	20 minutes

Pressure canning adjustments

Pressure canning requires that your food reach 240 degrees Fahrenheit. Additional pressure is needed in this case, as opposed to additional time.

The standard rule is to add 1 pound of pressure for each 1000 feet above sea level you are. However, you will rarely ever adjust more than 5 pounds, regardless of your elevation.

For safety reasons, pressure canners should never be used above 17 pounds of pressure.

Adjustments for Pressure Canning	
Altitude	Additional Pressure
1001-2000	+ 1
2001-4000	+ 3
4001-6000	+5
6001-8000	+5
8000-10,000	+5

For the recipes included in this book, times and pressures are given based on sea-level altitudes, so use these charts to adjust according to your location.

❧ We Be Jammin' ❧

Perhaps the very easiest thing to can is homemade jam. It's not very expensive, it's simple, and once you've made one kind of jam, others just cooperatively fall into place for you.

Jam is not only a delicious way to preserve a bounty of fruit – it provides a luxurious taste of summer during the cold winter months – a culinary treat to brighten up the taste of simple cornbread or biscuits.

So, if you're brand new to canning, this is the chapter for you. This is a wonderful way to get your feet wet and make something simple and delicious.

If you are going to all of the effort to make your own jams and jellies, please take the extra step of cleaning your produce carefully to remove pollutants, pesticides, and airborne contaminants. Instructions for this can be found on page 237.

Jam 101

For years, when I made jam, I reached for a box of pectin from the store. Then I spent some time reading up on store-bought pectin and I was very unhappy to discover the jams I'd been making for my family had been tainted with GMOs. I had unknowingly been contaminating the carefully sourced fruit and pricey turbinado sugar with the very things I strive to avoid, and I hadn't even given it a second thought.

Most brands exclaim breathlessly, "All natural pectin" or "Made from real fruit". And this is true - it does originate from fruit. Sounds okay, right? Don't be deceived. This misleading label makes it sound as though this is nothing more than some powdered fruit.

Here are the ingredients from the box of pectin lurking in my canning cupboard:

Dextrose, fruit pectin, citric acid

That doesn't sound too bad, right?

Wrong.

Dextrose is generally made from corn products (GMOs that are absolutely SOAKED in glyphosate). It is made from cornstarch, the main ingredient in good old High Fructose Corn Syrup.

Don't let anyone tell you that citric acid is "just Vitamin C". It is derived from GMO mold.

Not only does store-bought pectin contain unsavory ingredients, but it is also very highly processed. According to Wikipedia, this is how it is produced:

> The main raw materials for pectin production are dried citrus peel or apple pomace, both by-products of juice production. Pomace from sugar beet is also used to a small extent.

From these materials, pectin is extracted by adding hot dilute acid at pH-values from 1.5 – 3.5. During several hours of extraction, the protopectin loses some of its branching and chain length and goes into solution. After filtering, the extract is concentrated in vacuum and the pectin then precipitated by adding ethanol or isopropanol. An old technique of precipitating pectin with aluminium salts is no longer used (apart from alcohols and polyvalent cations, pectin also precipitates with proteins and detergents).

Alcohol-precipitated pectin is then separated, washed and dried. Treating the initial pectin with dilute acid leads to low-esterified pectins. When this process includes ammonium hydroxide, amidated pectins are obtained. After drying and milling, pectin is usually standardised with sugar and sometimes calcium salts or organic acids to have optimum performance in a particular application.

So, if you want to avoid GMOs and processed foods, what's a homemade-jam making mama to do?

Jam has been around for thousands of years. The first known book of jam recipes was written in Rome in the 1st century (source). Since I'm pretty sure our ancestors didn't have those handy little boxes of Sure-Jel or Certo sitting in their pantries, I set out to learn how they made a thick delicious preserve to spread on their biscuits.

My first attempt at breaking up with the box was to make my own pectin with green apples. While I ended up with a tasty product, it wasn't really jam-like. It's possible, considering the time of year, that the apples were too ripe to allow this to work for me, but I assume that unripe apples were not always available in the past when people wanted to make jam from the currently-ripe harvest.

I continued to read recipes and methods from days gone by. It soon became clear that adding pectin wasn't really necessary at all. In days past, the sugar and the fruit worked hand-in-hand to create the desired consistency.

I combined bits from a few different methods and finally came up with a jam that the entire family was happy with. In comparison with the boxed pectin jam, it doesn't gel quite as much, but after trying this jam, the texture of the other now seems slightly artificial to me. This produces a softer preserve with an incredibly intense fruit flavor. As well, when using this method, you don't get that layer of foam that you have to skim off the top like you do with the boxed pectin method.

The instructions for basic jams are all pretty much the same – you only need to make minor modifications for different fruits.

So, because we're all creative people, I'm laying out the general how-to, giving you a chart with special instructions fruit by fruit, and you can take it from there. This is followed by some specialty recipes.

Jam without Added Pectin

Ingredients:
- 7 pounds fresh or frozen fruit (approximately 14-20 cups)
- ¼ cup lemon or lime juice
- 5 cups + 2 tablespoons sugar
- Piece of clean cotton fabric for draining (I used a flour sack towel. This will be permanently stained, so don't use something you want to keep pretty.)

Directions:

1. Prepare your fruit. For berries, this means washing them and sorting them, removing little leaves and twigs, as well as berries that are shriveled. Leave the odd green berry in, because less ripe fruit has more naturally occurring pectin than ripe fruit. For fruits like apples or peaches, this might mean blanching and peeling them, then removing the cores.
2. Mash, finely chop, or puree your fruit. I used a blender to puree half of the fruit, and a food processor to finely chop the other half. We prefer a rough puree texture.
3. Pour this into a large crock or non-reactive bowl, layering your fruit with 3 of the cups of sugar. I use the ceramic insert from my crock-pot for this.

4. Leave the fruit and sugar mixture in your refrigerator overnight. The juice from the fruit will combine with the sugar and form a slightly jelled texture. Some liquid will separate from the sugar and fruit.
5. The next day, line a colander with a piece of fabric. Place the colander into a pot to catch the liquid from the fruit and sugar mixture. Pour your fruit and sugar mixture into the fabric-lined colander. Put this back in the refrigerator for at least an hour to drain. You can let it drain for longer with no ill effect – in fact this will result in an even thicker jam.

From this point on, you'll be making two separate products: jam and fruit syrup.

6. When you're ready to make jam, scoop the fruit out of the fabric-lined colander and place it in a pot with lots of open area to help it cook down faster. (This gives more space for the liquid to evaporate.)
7. The liquid that you caught in the other pot is the basis for your fruit syrup. You'll have about 1-2 pints of liquid. Place that on the stove and bring it to a rolling boil. Add 1/4 cup of sugar and a tbsp of lemon juice per pint and reduce heat to a simmer. I like to add one big spoonful of jam to this to add a little texture to the syrup.
8. Meanwhile, on another burner, bring your fruit and sugar mixture to a simmer, stirring frequently. After about an hour, the texture will have thickened. If you still have a great deal of liquid, you can use a fabric lined sieve to strain some more out. (You can add this liquid to the syrup.)
9. Fill sanitized jars with your products (syrup or jam). Process the water bath canner, according to the type of fruit you are canning and making adjustments for your altitude. (Refer to the chart for processing times.)

Jam with boxed pectin

If you wish to use boxed pectin to make your jam, here are the basic instructions for that process:

Directions:

1. Prep your fruit by washing it and cutting it up if necessary.

2. Smush your fruit. You can do this with a potato masher, food processer, blender, or food mill. For some fruits I like to puree them and have a smoother jam and for others I like chunkier jam – it's up to personal preference.
3. In a small bowl, use a fork to mix ¼ cup of the sugar with one packet of pectin.
4. In a saucepan, stir the fruit, lemon juice, and pectin together well.
5. Bring the mixture to a boil over medium heat, stirring frequently.
6. Once it is boiling, stir in the sugar and return to a boil for one minute.
7. This is important:

***

Jam Making Rule of Law:
Always test your jam!!!!

How?

You do this by keeping a spoon in the freezer - to test, drip a bit of the hot jam into the spoon to allow it to quick-cool - the consistency it reaches is the consistency your finished product will be.

At this point, I nearly always end up adding another 1/4 - 1/2 package of pectin - I use the cheaper pectin to "top it up" - return to a simmer for a couple of minutes and test again.

Omitting this step may result in a very tasty ice cream topping or waffle syrup, but not jam!
***

8. Ladle the jam carefully into your awaiting jars, wipe the rim, and cap your jars with snap lids and rings.
9. Process in a hot water bath canner, according to the ingredients chart.

FRUIT	SPECIAL INSTRUCTIONS	PROCESSING TIME
Apricot	Peel, slice in half to pit	5 minutes
Blackberry	optional step: mill to remove seeds	10 minutes
Blueberry	optional step: puree	7 minutes
Cherry	Pit with a cherry pitter, chop before cooking	10 minutes
Grape	Mill to remove seeds	10 minutes
Huckleberry	Check for stems	10 minutes
Peach	Peel, slice in half to remove pits	10 minutes
Plum	Slice in half to remove pits	5 minutes
Raspberry	Crush with a potato masher	10 minutes
Strawberry	Remove cores, mash with a potato masher	10 minutes

Blueberry-Lemon Jam

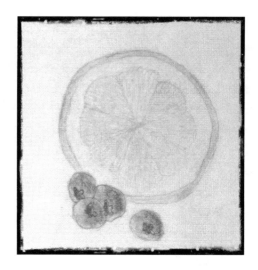

This stuff is like the Muse of Jams. Everyone that has tried it has been struck with sudden inspiration:

"OMGosh - can you imagine this on pancakes?"
"OMGosh - what if you used it on shortbread thumbprint cookies?"
"OMGosh - this needs good English scones!"

You get the idea.....you've gotta try it!

Ingredients:

- 7 to 8 pints fresh or frozen blueberries
- 3/4 cup lemon juice (or lime juice is also yummy)
- 5 cups sugar

Directions:

1. Wash and sort your berries. Look out for the little woody stems that like to hide in the berries and make sneaky unpleasant textures in your finished product.
2. Smush your berries. I like to use my Vitamix and puree the daylights out of them, but some people want more texture, in which case you could use a potato masher. (Warning - you will find berries behind the fridge, under the stove, beside the sink - I've even found

a couple in the bathroom since this project - those bad boys go everywhere!)

3. Pour your smushed berries into crock and layer them with 3 cups of the sugar. Top with ½ cup of lemon juice. Leave this in your fridge overnight.
4. The next day, place a fabric-lined colander in a bigger pot. Drain your berries-and-sugar for at least an hour.
5. When you're ready to make jam, scoop the fruit out of the fabric-lined colander and place it in a pot with lots of open area to help it cook down faster. (This gives more space for the liquid to evaporate.)
6. The liquid that you caught in the other pot is the basis for your fruit syrup. You'll have about 1-2 pints of liquid. Place that on the stove and bring it to a rolling boil. Add 1/4 cup of sugar and a tablespoon of lemon juice per pint and reduce heat to a simmer. I like to add one big spoonful of jam to this point to add a little texture to the syrup.
7. Meanwhile, on another burner, bring your fruit and sugar mixture to a simmer, stirring frequently. After about an hour, the texture will have thickened. If you still have a great deal of liquid, you can use a fabric lined sieve to strain some more out. (You can add this liquid to the syrup.)
8. Stir in 1/4 cups of lemon juice and 1 cup of sugar. Increase heat to get it simmering again.
9. When it has reached the desired texture, ladle the jam carefully into your awaiting jars, wipe the rim, and cap your jars with snap lids and rings. Ladle the syrup into jars, too.

Lid your jars and process them in a water bath canner for 7 minutes, adjusting for altitude. After allowing your little gems of blueberry-lemon jamgasm to cool, greedily hide them away so you don't have to share.

Dandelion Blossom Jam

If you are lucky enough to live in (or visit) an area that you are absolutely certain does not spray pesticides, you can join the bees and enjoy some Dandelion Nectar – except yours will be in the form of jam.

Set forth on an expedition to pick dandelions. You only need the tops – the yellow flowers – break them off right at the top of the stem. Pick 10-12 cups worth of blossoms. Your kids will think it is great fun initially, but then they'll get bored and you will have to pick the rest.

I haven't been able to make this successfully without added pectin. I recommend Pomona Pectin for this recipe.

Ingredients:

- 10-12 cups dandelion blossoms
- 4 ½ cups sugar
- 2 tablespoons lemon juice
- 1 packet Pomona pectin or pectin of your choice

Directions:

1. Prepare the blossoms by pinching them between your fingers and snipping off the green part with scissors.
2. Place the petals in a large glass bowl and cover them with 4 cups of boiling water. That's it for today – you're going to sleep while the petals brew up a golden yellow dandelion tea at room temperature.
3. The next morning, drain the tea through a coffee filter into another container. You should have 3-4 cups of dandelion tea.
4. (Now is the time to put a wet spoon into the freezer for jam testing!)
5. Pour the strained tea into a saucepan and stir in the lemon juice.
6. Follow the instructions on your pectin package.
7. Test your jam – if the consistency is right, remove it from the heat, and immediately ladle it into sanitized jars.
8. Lid your jars and process them in a water bath canner for 10 minutes, adjusting for altitude.

You'll be left with a topaz-toned honey-like substance that will give you a new understanding of the minds of bees.

Spiced Cherry Amaretto Jam

Ingredients:

- 4 pounds washed sweet cherries (like Bings)
- 4 ½ cups sugar
- ½ cup lemon juice
- ¼ cup amaretto
- ¼ teaspoon salt
- 1 teaspoon ground cinnamon
- ½ teaspoon ground cloves
- ¼ teaspoon allspice
- ¼ teaspoon ground nutmeg

Directions:

1. Using a cherry pitter, remove the pits from the cherries
2. In batches, use your food processor to roughly chop the cherries.

3. (Unlike most pectin-free recipes, the cherries don't need to sit overnight or be drained, unless you want to)
4. Place the cherries into a saucepan and stir in amaretto, lemon juice, salt, and spices.
5. Bring the mixture to a boil, then reduce heat and simmer it until you've reached the desired consistency.
6. Ladle the hot jam into sanitized pint jars, allowing ¼ inch of headspace.
7. Lid the jars and process in a water bath canner for 10 minutes, adjusting for altitude.

Ginger Peach Jam

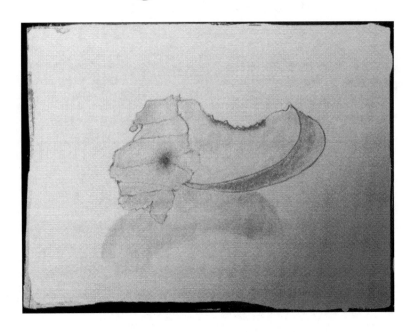

It's like a taste of summer with a peppery bite! You will NOT want to share, so plan to make a second batch for gifts!

(Note: peaches can be peeled just like tomatoes – blanch them for a minute in boiling water, then drop them into ice water, and the skin will slide right off!)

Ingredients:

- 6 pounds peeled, chopped peaches
- 2 inch piece ginger, grated, or 2 teaspoons powdered ginger
- ¼ cup lemon juice
- 1 teaspoon ground cinnamon
- 1 teaspoon nutmeg
- 5 cups sugar

Directions:

1. Prep your peaches by blanching them in hot water, then dipping them in an ice bath to remove the peel. Then remove the pit.
2. Mash or roughly puree the peaches. Layer them with 3 cups of sugar in a crock and place them in the fridge overnight.
3. Using a fabric-lined colander over a bowl, drain the puree for 3 hours.
4. In a large saucepan, bring to a drained peaches, ginger, cinnamon, and nutmeg. Reduce heat and simmer.
5. (Smell that peachy spicy goodness? Mmmmm…hey – no tasting!)
6. Meanwhile, in another pot, simmer your peach juice with ¼ cup of sugar per pint. You can added a little vanilla extract to the syrup for a different flavor.
7. Add the other cup of the sugar to the jam, stirring well, and simmer until it reaches the consistency you prefer.
8. When it is the consistency you like, ladle it into your sanitized jars.
9. Process the jars in a water bath canner for 10 minutes, adjusting for altitude.

CrockPot Plum Butter

This is an incredibly simple, hands-off recipe that requires practically no attention from you from the time you put it in the crockpot until the time you put it in jars for canning! Meanwhile, it selflessly makes your home smell wonderful while you ignore it.

Ingredients:

- 14 pounds plums
- 4 cups sugar
- 2 tablespoons pure vanilla extract
- 1 teaspoon nutmeg

Directions:

1. Follow the instructions on page 237 to remove pesticides, etc., from the skin of the plums.
2. Once they are clean, slice your plums in half, remove the stone, and toss them in the crockpot.
3. Once your plums are in the crock, stir in the sugar.
4. Set the crockpot on low, put the lid askew, and cook for about 10 hours, or until the plum butter has reached the desired thickness. (Keep in mind it will thicken a tiny bit more as it cools.)
5. Once the proper consistency has been reached, add the vanilla, stirring well to infiltrate the entire batch with the deliciousness of it. (Adding the vanilla earlier in the process will cause the vanilla to dissipate as the plums cook down – it's much better when you add it at the end.)
6. Ladle the plum butter into pint jars. (You will have approximately 8 jars full.)
7. Process in a hot water bath canner for 10 minutes, adjusting for altitude.

Karak's Maker's Mark Fig Jam

The friend that inspired me to start an organic garden also provided me with the recipe for her infamous MM Fig Jam. Blessed with a fig tree in her amazing urban garden, she has so much fun canning this concoction that I decided it had to be included here.

Ingredients:

- 8 pounds fresh figs
- Juice of 3 lemons & zest
- ½ cup lemon juice (add this to be on the safe side of the acid scale)
- 2 cups sugar
- 1 packet no-sugar-needed pectin
- ½ cup water
- 1 ½ cups Maker's Mark bourbon (adjust to your taste)

Directions:

1. Wash figs and remove stems. Place them into a large sauce pan and bring them to a simmer.
2. Simmer them over a low heat for about an hour to cook them down, stirring occasionally.
3. Stir in lemon ingredients, water, pectin, and sugar and bring to a boil.
4. With a candy thermometer, check the temperature, and once figs have reached 220 degrees, add the Maker's Mark.
5. Ladle the hot jam into sanitized jars.
6. Process the jars for 13 minutes, adjusting for altitude.

Raspberry Jalapeno Jam

In my mind, there isn't much that's better than sweet and spicy at the same time. This makes the juxtaposition of raspberries and jalapenos a match made in sweet-spicy heaven.

Every year at Christmas, I dump this out over a block of cream cheese and serve it with crackers. I could honestly just eat that and nothing else, although people seem to frown on guests that don't eat some of the turkey.

This jam makes a lovely and elegant appetizer, a glaze for chicken or fish, and a delightful condiment on a turkey and Swiss cheese sandwich.

Ingredients:

- 8 cups raspberries
- 2-4 jalapeno peppers
- 4 cups sugar
- ¼ cup lemon juice

Directions:

1. Prep the raspberries by washing them gently. Then place them in the food processor and roughly puree them.
2. In a large bowl, layer the raspberry puree with 2 cups of sugar. Leave this in the refrigerator overnight. The next morning there won't be very much juice – you most likely will not have enough to make syrup.
3. Carefully prep your jalapenos by wearing gloves, mask and hazmat suit. (Okay, not really, but be careful cause those suckers really make you burn if you touch your face after playing with them.) I use the food processer to get teeny tiny bits of jalapeno without massive pain and pepper juice exposure.
4. Stir raspberries, peppers and lemon juice together in a large pot, bringing the mixture to a simmer.
5. Gradually stir in the other 2 cups sugar and allow it to simmer until it reaches the desired texture.
6. When it is the proper consistency, ladle it into your ready-and-waiting sterilized jars.
7. Process in a water bath canner for 10 minutes, adjusting for altitude.

Variation:

You can pair jalapenos with many different fruits. I've successfully married hot peppers with blackberries and peaches and the result has been delicious. (A special spicy peach recipe follows.)

Sweet and Spicy Pepper Peach Jam

This is another holiday favorite at our house. I use half pint jars, which contain the perfect amount to pour over cream cheese, yogurt cheese, or baked Brie. This sophisticated appetizer is best served with simple, hearty crackers. Trust me, you'll look fancy when you serve it!

The recipe is identical to the Brown Sugar Peach Preserves that follows, aside from the addition of jalapenos at the end. In fact, you can ladle out your preserves into jars and then add jalapenos to the remaining jam for two flavors in one batch.

Ingredients

- 6 pounds fresh peaches
- 2 cups white or Turbinado sugar
- 2 cups brown or Muscovado sugar
- ¼ cup lemon juice
- 1/4 cup finely chopped jalapeno peppers - include seeds for a spicier flavor

Directions:

1. Prep your fruit by washing it carefully. If the peaches are not organic, make a baking soda rinse to help remove the pesticides. (page 237)
2. Smush your fruit. You can do this with a potato masher, food processer, blender, or food mill. For this particular jam, I like to puree most of the fruit (including the skins) and then finely chop some of the fruit for added texture.
3. Layer the peaches and the white sugar in a large crock and leave it overnight in the refrigerator. The next day, drain the peaches using a fabric lined colander over a large bowl for at least 2 hours.
4. In a stockpot, stir the peach puree, peach chunks, and lemon juice together well.
5. Bring the mixture to a boil over medium heat, stirring frequently.
6. Once it is boiling, stir in the jalapenos and the brown sugar and reduce it to a simmer, being sure to stir frequently, until it reaches the desired consistency.
7. Ladle the jam carefully into your awaiting (sanitized) jars, wipe the rims, and cap your jars with snap lids and rings.
8. Process in a water bath canner for 10 minutes and make adjustments for your altitude.

Brown Sugar Peach Preserves

Ingredients:

- 6 pounds fresh peaches
- 2 cups white or Turbinado sugar
- 2 cups brown or Muscavado sugar
- ¼ cup lemon juice

Directions:

1. Prep your fruit by washing it carefully. If the peaches are not organic, make a baking soda rinse to help remove the pesticides. (page 237)
2. Smush your fruit. You can do this with a potato masher, food processer, blender, or food mill. For this particular jam, I like to puree most of the fruit (including the skins) and then finely chop some of the fruit for added texture.
3. Layer the peaches and the white sugar in a large crock and leave it overnight in the refrigerator. The next day, drain the peaches using a fabric lined colander over a large bowl for at least 2 hours.
4. In a stockpot, stir the peach puree, peach chunks, and lemon juice together well.

5. Bring the mixture to a boil over medium heat, stirring frequently.
6. Once it is boiling, stir in the brown sugar, reduce it to a simmer, being sure to stir frequently, until it reaches the desired consistency.
7. Ladle the jam carefully into your awaiting (sanitized) jars, wipe the rims, and cap your jars with snap lids and rings.
8. Process in a water bath canner for 10 minutes and make adjustments for your altitude.

Just Call Me Condimental

Condiment [ˈkɒndɪmənt]

n

A condiment is an edible substance, such as sauce or seasoning, added to food to impart a particular flavor, enhance its flavor, or in some cultures, to complement the dish.

You can make the simplest fare tastier, more elegant, and even more nutritious with the right condiment. I'm not talking about squirting ketchup on a burger – I'm talking about a mouth-watering relish made of garden vegetables, a surprisingly luscious fruit salsa, or a sweet-n-savory chutney to turn things instantly gourmet.

The condiments all have an acidity level that allows for water bath canning, unless otherwise noted.

Having shelves full of chutneys and relishes will add a boost of nutrition and flavor to your meals. As well, many chutneys are of the "kitchen sink" variety, which means that you can use up those odds and ends of produce that are not quite enough to make a full batch of a single item.

When your garden is producing more than you can eat, consider preserving some as condiments to add to the variety on your groaning pantry shelves.

Relishes
&
Chutneys

A Dilly of a Relish

Ingredients:

- 6 pounds pickling cucumbers
- ½ cup pickling salt
- 2 teaspoons turmeric
- 3 cups water
- 2 large onions, finely chopped
- 4 cloves finely minced garlic
- 1/3 cup white sugar
- 2 tablespoons dill seed
- 3 cups white vinegar

Directions:

1. Using a food processor or a grinder, finely chop cucumbers.
2. Place chopped cucumbers in a glass bowl, sprinkle with salt and turmeric, and cover with water for 2 hours.
3. Drain cucumbers and rinse in a colander under cold water, squeezing out the excess water with your hands.

4. Combine cucumbers, onions, garlic, sugar, dill seed, and white vinegar in a saucepan and bring to a boil.
5. Reduce heat and simmer 10 minutes.
6. Ladle into jars leaving ½ inch headspace.
7. Process in a water bath canner for 15 minutes, adjusting for altitude.

Holy Jalapeno Relish

Hot peppers are the evil vindictive uncles of the vegetable garden family. Handle them with care because when you cut them up, they fight back. Use rubber gloves and do not rub your eyes, nose, mouth, or any other mucous membrane (that I don't want to hear) about after handling them. Most of the heat is in the seeds. Use or do not use the seeds accordingly to turn up (or down) the heat in your finished product.

Ingredients:

- 5 pounds jalapeno peppers
- 2 cups sugar
- 4 cups white vinegar
- ½ cup cilantro leaves (optional)

(Another option, if you want a condiment with less heat, is to replace up to half of the jalapenos with green bell peppers.)

Directions:

1. In a food processor, finely chop the peppers. Don't turn them into a pureed mush – make them the consistency of relish.
2. Meanwhile, in a large cooking pot, stir the sugar into the vinegar and bring to a boil.
3. Immediately reduce the heat and stir in your hot peppers.
4. Use your food processor to chop the cilantro leaves, if you are using them, then stir them into your relish.
5. Bring the relish back to a boil, reduce heat, and simmer for 5 minutes until heated through.
6. Ladle the relish into pint jars allowing ½ inch of head space.
7. Process the jars in a water bath canner for 10 minutes, adjusting for altitude.

Use this to top up the heat on anything you'd like to have spicier. It's great on chili, tacos, sausages, etc.! This relish gets a workout at our house because some family members like spicy food and some do not, so we can customize the heat to suit ourselves.

Southern Belle Kitchen Sink Chow-Chow

The beauty of this recipe is the fine art of making something delicious out of something that you have running out your ears in any combination that suits your overflow situation at the time.

Ingredients:
- 8 cups assorted veggies (zucchini, green tomatoes, cabbage, summer squash, cauliflower - whatever you've got)
- 1 cup onion, finely chopped
- 1 cup red bell pepper, diced
- ¼ cup finely minced jalapeno pepper

Brine:
- 2 cups apple cider vinegar
- 2 cups brown or white sugar
- 2 teaspoon dry mustard powder
- 1 teaspoon turmeric
- 1 teaspoon powdered ginger

In a spice bag or piece of cheesecloth:
- 2 teaspoons each celery seed, whole white mustard seeds, and coriander seeds
- 2 whole allspice seeds
- 3 whole cloves

Directions:

1. Place all veggies in a colander over a bowl and sprinkle them with salt. Leave this in the fridge overnight – this will remove the extra moisture.
2. Zzzzzzzzz…..
3. In a large stock pot (non-reactive) mix well the ingredients for the brine and toss in the spice bag.
4. Bring it to a boil then drop it to a simmer for 10 minutes, stirring often, to dissolve the sugar.
5. Stir in the veggies and heat through.
6. Ladle this mixture into jars no larger than 1 pint, leaving a half inch of headspace.
7. Lid the jars and process in a water bath canner for 10 minutes, depending on altitude.

Chow-chow is generally served in the South as a condiment for pinto beans or field peas, alongside a chunk of cornbread. However, it lends a sweet spicy crunch to any simple fare.

Sweet-As-Can-Be Relish

Brighten up your burgers with this sweet and simple cucumber relish. Once you test the freshness of your own relish, you will never eat the food-color and HFCS-laden grocery store relish again!

Ingredients:

- 4 pounds pickling cucumbers
- 2 cups diced red bell pepper
- 2 cups finely chopped white onion
- ½ cup pickling salt
- 1/2 cups white vinegar
- 2 1/3 cups granulated sugar
- 4 tablespoons mustard seeds
- 2 tablespoons celery seeds

Directions:

1. Using a food processor or grinder, finely chop the cucumbers.
2. Place the cucumbers in a large glass bowl and stir in the salt. Allow them to sit on the counter at room temperature for 4 hours.
3. Drain cucumbers and rinse in a colander under cold water, squeezing out the excess water with your hands.
4. Combine, garlic, sugar, mustard seeds, celery seeds, and white vinegar in a saucepan and bring to a boil.
5. Reduce heat and stir in cucumbers, onions, and peppers, then return to a full boil.
6. Reduce heat and simmer the mixture for 10 minutes.
7. Ladle the hot relish into pint or half pint jars, allowing ½ inch of headspace.
8. Lid the jars and process in a hot water bath canner for 10 minutes, adjusting for altitude.

British "Branston Pickle"

CC, my bestie from the UK, introduced me to this deliciousness! This sweet and sour condiment makes excellent use of random bits of garden produce. It is especially complimentary to dishes made with cheddar cheese or bleu cheese.

Ingredients:

- 4 cups diced peeled rutabaga
- 1 head cauliflower
- 3 carrots
- 2 onions
- 2 small zucchinis
- 2 Granny Smith apples, peeled and cored
- 1 cup chopped dates
- 12 gherkin pickles
- 5 cloves garlic, minced
- 1 cup packed brown sugar
- 2-2/3 cups malt vinegar
- 2-1/2 cups water
- 1/3 cup lemon juice
- 1/4 cup Worcestershire sauce
- 2 teaspoons salt

- 2 teaspoons mustard seeds
- 1-1/2 teaspoons ground allspice
- 1/4 teaspoon cayenne pepper

Directions:

1. Using a food processor, finely chop the first 9 ingredients in batches.
2. Pour the veggies into a large saucepan and stir in sugar, vinegar, water, lemon juice, Worcestershire sauce, salt, mustard seeds, allspice and cayenne pepper.
3. Bring the mixture to a boil, then pour into a crock pot and cook on low for 4-6 hours, with the lid askew, until the sauce has reached the desired consistency.
4. Ladle into pint jars, allowing ½ inch of headspace.
5. Lid your jars and process a water bath canner for 15 minutes, based on altitude.

Salsas

Sassy Salsa Fresca

Ingredients:

- 8 pounds tomatoes (see tomato prep on page 229)
- 4 cups bell peppers, seeded and chopped
- ½ cup jalapeno peppers, with center removed (leave in seeds for super-spicy salsa, reduce amount of jalapenos for milder salsa)
- 5 cups chopped onion
- 1 ½ cups lemon or lime juice
- 4 cloves garlic
- 4-6 tablespoons fresh cilantro leaves (if you HATE cilantro, you're weird, but use parsley instead)
- 1 teaspoon chili powder
- 1 can tomato paste (optional)

You can use a food processor to make this quicker or you can hand chop every single bit of it – it's all up to your personal combination of time and laziness.

Directions:

1. Using your food processor, add the tomatoes, peppers, onion, garlic, and cilantro a batch at a time. Process on the "chop" function until you've reached the desired chunkiness, then pour each batch into a large stockpot.
2. Once all of your veggies are in the pot, stir in your lemon or lime juice, chili powder, and tomato paste (if you're using it).
3. Bring your mixture to a gentle simmer – you aren't trying to cook the ingredients – you are just getting it warm so that it processes correctly in the water bath. (At this point I always taste a little sample to be sure the flavor doesn't require adjustment.)
4. Ladle the warm salsa into the prepared jars that are eagerly awaiting it.
5. Wipe the lip of the jars, place the flats and rings on them, and lift them into the vigorously boiling water bath.
6. Process for 15 minutes, adjusting for altitude.

It's Easy Being Green Tomato Salsa

This can be mixed with a basic white sauce to create the best enchilada sauce on the planet!

Ingredients:

- 7 cups green tomatoes (see tomato prep on page 229– green tomatoes can be prepped exactly like ripe tomatoes)
- 3 jalapeno peppers
- 1 green bell pepper
- 2 large onions
- 3 cloves garlic
- ½ cup lime juice
- ½ cup of cilantro
- 2 teaspoons ground cumin
- 1 teaspoon salt

Directions:

1. Using a food processor, chop tomatoes, peppers, onions, and garlic until they reach the desired chunkiness.
2. Pour the processed veggies into a large stock pot. Stir in cilantro, cumin, salt and lime juice.
3. Bring to a boil, then reduce heat and simmer for 5 minutes
4. Ladle green salsa into your ready-n-waiting pint jars, leaving a half inch of headspace at the top.
5. Process the jars in a water bath canner for 20, adjusting for altitude.

Peachy-Keen Salsa

This sweet-and-spicy salsa is mouth-watering over rice, chicken, or fish. Pop a bow on this pretty little jar of peachy goodness for a lovely and elegant homemade gift.

Ingredients:

- 8 cups chopped, peeled peaches
- 1 large red onion, finely chopped
- 4-6 jalapeno peppers, seeded and finely chopped
- 1 red bell pepper, diced
- 6 cloves garlic, finely minced
- ½ cup cilantro
- 1 tablespoon cumin
- ½ cup apple cider vinegar
- 1 cup sugar

Directions:

1. In a large stockpot combine all the ingredients except the sugar.
2. Combine well and bring to a boil.
3. Stir in the sugar and return to a boil – boil for one minute.
4. Ladle the salsa into your prepared jars.
5. Process your Peachy-Keen Salsa in a water bath canner for 15 minutes, adjusting for altitude.

Getting
Saucy

The REAL Tomato Ketchup

Once you try this taste-of-summer condiment, those little packets and squirt bottles will never satisfy your ketchup craving again. This is a big project but it will keep you (and possibly your neighbours and friends) in the red stuff for a year. Using your blender will definitely speed things along.

Ingredients:

- 12 pounds Roma or other paste type tomatoes
- 1 pound onions, quartered
- 1/2 pound sweet red peppers, sliced into strips
- 1/2 pound sweet green peppers, sliced into strips
- 4-1/2 cups cider vinegar
- 2 cups brown sugar
- 2 tablespoons pickling salt
- 1 tablespoon dry mustard
- ½ tablespoon crushed chili peppers
- 1/4 teaspoon ground allspice
- 1/2 tablespoon ground cloves
- 1/4 teaspoon ground cinnamon

Directions:

1. Prepare your tomatoes as per the Tomato Prep on page 229.
2. Using your blender, puree your tomatoes, peppers and onions – you will have to do numerous batches. Pour each pureed batch into a large stock pot.
3. Bring the mixture to a boil, then reduce heat and simmer it for one hour, uncovered.
4. Stir in the vinegar and spices and then pour the entire mixture into your crockpot. You are going to cook this on low heat for about 12 hours UNCOVERED. My crockpot is oval so I always put the lid on sideways to retain a bit of the heat but still allow the steam to escape. This will allow the concoction to "cook down" and get thick.
5. Zzzzzzzzz.....
6. Once the ketchup is at your preferred consistency, ladle it into pint jars.
7. Lid the jars and process them in a water bath for 15, adjusting for altitude.

Renegade Taco Sauce

I invented this sauce when a racoon did a night raid on my tomato patch. The Renegade Raccoon took a bite out of some newly ripe tomatoes and knocked some green ones to the ground. This was my effort to salvage them and it was so good that it has become a regular item in my pantry. (I decided that Raccoon Taco Sauce might bring up some unsavoury mental images, and thus named it Renegade Taco sauce.) That is a long way to say, you can include up to 1 pound of green tomatoes without any change to the product.

Ingredients:

- 3 pounds tomatoes (see tomato prep on page 229)
- 1 large bell pepper
- 3 cloves garlic
- ½ cup white vinegar
- 2-6 jalapenos
- 1 large onion
- 1 can tomato paste
- 3 tablespoons chili powder
- 1 tablespoon cumin
- ¼ cup cilantro leaves
- 1 teaspoon salt

Directions:

1. Use your food processor and puree the tomatoes, peppers, garlic, cilantro leaves, and onions.
2. Pour the puree into a stock pot and stir in the remaining ingredients.
3. Bring the sauce to a boil and then reduce the heat. Simmer for 10 minutes, stirring frequently.
4. Taste time – check to see if the spices need adjustment.
5. Ladle the hot sauce into pint jars.
6. Process the jars in a hot water bath for 20 minutes, adjusting for altitude.

Honey Vidalia BBQ Sauce

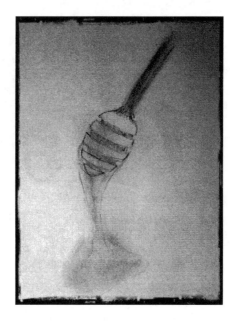

Your barbecues will never be the same – people will clamor for a jar of this sauce to take home – you might want to consider making a double batch and doling the extras out for Christmas!

Ingredients:

- 15 cups prepped Roma tomatoes (see page 229)
- 2 cups Vidalia (or other sweet) onion
- 2 cups red bell pepper
- 6 cloves crushed garlic
- 1½ cups honey
- 1 ½ cups apple cider vinegar
- 1 tablespoon dry mustard
- 1 tablespoon smoked Hungarian paprika
- 1 tablespoon canning salt
- 1 teaspoon black pepper
- 1 teaspoon cayenne pepper

Directions:

1. Using a blender or food processor, puree tomatoes, onions, peppers and garlic.
2. Pour the puree into a large stock pot and stir in all other ingredients.
3. Bring to a boil until honey is well-absorbed, then pour the mixture into your crockpot.
4. Taste test to see if your seasonings need any adjustment.
5. With the lid on sideways or askew so steam can escape, cook the sauce down for about 4-6 hours, stirring every once in a while. Check your consistency and keep in mind it will thicken up a little more as it cools.
6. Ladle the sauce into your prepared jars, leaving ½ inch of headspace.
7. Process in a pressure bath for 20 minutes, adjusting for altitude.

Cha-Cha Chili Sauce

This complex sauce is sweet and spicy and tangy all at once. It's a delightful topping for all things savory, and especially nice when the cold sauce contrasts against a hot food. All good Southerners know that pinto beans are not pinto beans without a little bit of chili sauce on top!

Ingredients:

- 10 cups prepped ripe tomatoes
- 2 cups chopped white onions
- 2 cups green bell peppers
- 2 cups chopped, peeled, plums
- 2 very finely diced jalapenos
- 1 ½ cups brown sugar
- 2 cups apple cider vinegar
- 5 teaspoons salt
- 2 tablespoons pickling spices (in a spice bag)
- 2 cups vinegar
- 1 teaspoon cinnamon
- 1 teaspoon dry mustard

Directions:

1. Coarsely chop the tomatoes, reserving juice.
2. Combine all ingredients in a crockpot and cook on low for 4-6 hours, with the lid askew to allow steam to escape.
3. Once the sauce has reached the desired consistency, ladle it into hot pint jars.
4. Lid your jars and process in a water bath canner for 15 minutes, adjusting for altitude.

❧ Pickles with Pizazz ❧

Dill-icious Sour Pickles

Ingredients:

- 45-50 cucumbers, about 3"-4" in length

Brine:

- 1 ½ cups white vinegar
- cups water
- 1/3 cup pickling salt

For each jar:

- 1 grape leaf (the tannin helps keep the pickles crisp)
- 2 heads of dill
- 2 cloves of garlic, crushed

Directions:

1. Scrub your cucumbers with a vegetable brush, then soak them in an ice water bath for 2-6 hours.
2. Combine the ingredients for the brine and bring them to a rolling boil for 5 minutes.
3. Meanwhile, place a grape leaf in the bottom of each jar. (If you don't have access to grape leaves there are commercial stay-crisp additives on the market – I personally prefer the natural options whenever possible.)
4. Then add your other ingredients to the jar – approximately 6-8 pickles per pint, the dill and the garlic. You can process the cucumbers whole or cut them into spears, depending on your personal preference.
5. Pour the hot brine over the contents of each jar.
6. Lid your jars and process in a water bath canner for 10 minutes.
7. Remove the jars *immediately* from the canner for a more crisp pickle.

I Like Bread and Butterrrrr Pickles

(You have to sing that song when making these pickles – it's the rule!)

Ingredients:

- 5-7 pounds 4- to 6-inch cucumbers, cut into 1/4-inch slices
- 2 pounds white onion, thinly sliced into rings
- 1/2 cup canning salt

Brine:

- 3 cups white vinegar
- 2 cups white sugar
- 2 tablespoons mustard seed
- 2 teaspoons turmeric
- 2 teaspoons celery seed
- 1 teaspoon ginger powder
- 1 teaspoon peppercorns

Optional:

- 1 grape leaf for each jar

Directions:

1. Place cucumber and onion slices in a large glass bowl, layering with pickling salt.
2. Cover the salted veggies with ice cubes and allow them to stand in the refrigerator for 2 hours.
3. Drain them in a colander, then rinse them and drain them again.
4. Combine the brine ingredients in a large saucepot; bring to a boil.
5. Pack your sanitized jars with one grape leaf in the bottom of each (if using), topped by the cucumbers and onions.
6. Pack hot pickles and liquid into hot jars, 1/2-inch headspace.
7. Pour the hot brine over the contents of your jars.
8. Lid the jars and process 10 minutes, adjusting for altitude.

Southern-style Sweet Pickles

Ingredients:

- 8 pounds of 3- to 4-inch long pickling cucumbers (whole)
- 1/3 cup canning or pickling salt

Syrup:

- 4-1/2 cups white sugar
- 3-1/2 cups white vinegar
- 2 teaspoons celery seed
- 3 tablespoons of pickling spice

Per jar:

- 1 grape leaf

Directions:

1. Place scrubbed cucumbers in a large glass bowl, layering with pickling salt.
2. Cover the salted veggies with ice cubes and allow them to stand in the refrigerator for 2 hours.
3. Drain them in a colander, then rinse them and drain them again.

4. In a large saucepan, combine syrup ingredients and bring them to a boil.
5. Cut off the hard ends of the cucumbers and pack them into jars, atop a grape leaf.
6. Pour hot syrup over the contents of the jars, leaving ½ inch of headspace.
7. Process in a hot water bath canner for 10 minutes, removing the jars *immediately* when the processing time is up.

Random Pickled Veggies

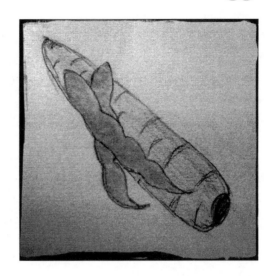

At the end of the season, when you have too much produce left in your garden to eat right away, but not enough to can any one thing, make yourself some Random Pickled Veggies to enjoy throughout the winter. The ingredients list is flexible – it's actually more of an ingredients *suggestion* list - go with what you have, just try to keep the total sum of veggies the same.

Ingredients:

- 1 pound zucchini, cut into ¼ inch slices
- 1 pound green or yellow beans, ends removed
- 1 pound carrots, cut into ¼ inch coins
- 1 pound baby pearl onions, peeled *or* 1 pound of white onion, thinly sliced into rings
- 2 bell peppers, any color, cut into strips

Brine:

- 3 cups apple cider vinegar
- 2 cups brown sugar
- 2 tablespoons dry mustard
- 2 tablespoons whole mustard seed
- 1 ½ tablespoons pickling salt

- 1 teaspoon ground cinnamon
- 1 teaspoon ground ginger
- (optional) hot peppers of choice, sliced lengthwise

Directions:

1. Combine all veggies in a large bowl and set aside.
2. Combine the contents of the brine in a large saucepan and bring the mixture to a boil.
3. Stir in the veggies and return to a boil. Reduce heat and simmer for 15 minutes.
4. Pack veggies and liquid into pint jars, allowing ½ inch of headspace.
5. Lid the jars and process for 15 minutes, adjusting for altitude.

Pleasantly Pickled Red Onions

Pickled onions are milder and sweeter than just topping a burger or sandwich with a slice of raw onion, and they're far more elegant. They are also a lovely addition to a salad - you hardly need dressing when you have these babies with a little of the liquid drizzled over your greens.

Ingredients:

- 2 cups red wine vinegar
- 2 cloves garlic, smashed
- 1 whole clove
- ¼ cup brown sugar
- 5 cups thinly sliced rings of red onion

Directions:

1. Thinly slice red onion.
2. Cry.
3. Once you can see again, in a saucepan, bring vinegar, garlic, clove and brown sugar to a boil then immediately reduce heat and simmer for 5 minutes
4. Dip out the large pieces of garlic and discard.

5. Stir the onions into the pot and return to a boil, stirring constantly.
6. Reduce heat and simmer until the onions are soft (about 5 minutes).
7. Ladle the onions into pint jars and disperse liquid evenly throughout the jars, allowing ½ inch of headspace.
8. Lid the jars and process them in a water bath canner for 10 minutes, adjusting for altitude.

❧ Fruit Frenzy ❧

Fruit is loaded with vitamins, including vitamin C. A lack of vitamin C for an extended period of time will cause the deficiency disease scurvy.

Scurvy starts out with symptoms of paleness, lethargy, and feelings of depression. If the deficiency is not corrected, the sufferer will begin bleeding from the gums and other mucus membranes. As it worsens tooth loss, jaundice, neuropathy and eventually, death, occur.

Imagine the grocery store is no longer an option – where are you going to get your sources of important nutrients? You will need to have them preserved and waiting on your shelves.

When the fruit trees are groaning with their bounty, take a break from biting into those fresh, juicy peaches and store up some jars of sunshine for the winter.

How 'Bout THOSE Apples Apple Sauce

When life gives you apples, make apple sauce!

This recipe is perfect for baby food because it has only 2 ingredients. Apples and water. None of that nasty high-fructose-corn-syrup slop in THIS apple sauce!

Because of my inherent laziness, I used the "blender method" of making applesauce. This is the "easy" method. Shoot me if I one day have to do the difficult method because this was almost 3 hours of hands-on work.

Think about how much work it would be to do this manually and cook down the apples then put them through an apple sauce mill! Anyhow, I digress. The blender method: it requires far less cooking time and does not require you to peel the apples, both of which help to keep the vitamin content high. If you are leaving the peel on it is especially important to clean the fruit carefully (see page 237).

Ingredients:

- 1 bushel cleaned apples (see page 237)
- Water as needed

Directions:

1. Chop and core the apples.
2. Using a blender or food processor, puree the apples, skins and all, with just enough water to allow the blender to work.
3. Do this in batches and then pour the puree into a large stock pot.
4. Cook the sauce only long enough to heat it up.
5. As soon as the apple sauce is merrily bubbling away, it's hot enough to ladle into your prepared jars. Be sure to allow at least ½ inch of headspace.
6. Lid your jars and process in a water bath canner for 20-25-30 minutes, based on altitude.

Spiced Apple Sauce

If you'd like a little more flavor in your apple sauce, this will fit the bill. I can't even express how great your house will smell while this simmers on the stove. No sugar is needed for this batch of fragrant deliciousness.

Ingredients:

- 1 bushel apples
- lemon juice as needed
- 1/2 cup cinnamon
- 1/8 cup powdered ginger
- 2 tablespoons allspice
- 1 tablespoon powdered cloves

Directions:

1. Prep your apples by removing the pesticide as directed on page 237.
2. Core the apples and cut them into chunks.
3. Using your blender or food processor, puree your apple chunks in batches. Add enough lemon juice to each batch to allow it to puree.
4. Pour the puree into the stock pot. Stir in all of the spices and bring to a light simmer. You aren't cooking the applesauce; you are merely *heating* it.

5. Lean over the pot and smmmmmeeeeellllllll how fantastic that spiced applesauce smells. Do not skip this vital step or your entire applesauce making process will be disrupted and the entire batch could fail based on this alone.
6. Pour the hot applesauce into your prepared jars. Clean off the lip of the jar and top it with a snap lid and a ring.
7. Process your apple sauce in a hot water bath canner for 20-25-30 minutes.

Cranberry Apple Slices

These jars of goodness simple beg and plead to be topped with a crisp crumb topping, baked, and then smothered in vanilla ice cream. Of course you can also grab a spoon and dig in right from the jar! Because of the tartness of the cranberries, I do add sugar, however, it's only two cups divided across 6 quarts.

(Note: If you happen to fall into a pile of pears, they are equally delicious preserved this way!)

Ingredients:

- 6 pounds apples (pesticide removed as per recommendations on page 237)
- 3 cups cranberries
- Bowl of lemon juice (for dipping apples)
- 5 cups apple juice
- 2 cups brown sugar
- 6 cinnamon sticks
- 6 cloves

Directions:

1. Core and slice apples, dipping them immediately in lemon juice (to prevent browning)
2. Meanwhile bring apple juice and brown sugar to a boil.
3. Carefully pour apple slices and cranberries into boiling juice and simmer for 5 minutes.
4. Place 1 cinnamon stick and 1 clove into each quart jar, then ladle fruit mixture and liquids into jars.
5. Make sure there are no air pockets, lid the jars, and process in a water bath canner for 25-30-35 minutes, based on altitude.

Spiced Mulled Pears
(Non-alcoholic)

As a break from regular sliced pears, try this decadently spiced version. This looks elegant and difficult, but honestly, it couldn't be easier! If you don't have all of the spices listed here, just double up on the ones you do have – versatility!

Ingredients:

- 8-10 very firm pears
- 4 cups red grape juice
- 1 cup orange juice
- ½ cup brown sugar
- 2 tablespoons pure vanilla extract
- 6 star anise pods
- 6 cinnamon sticks
- 12 whole cloves
- 12 black peppercorns

Directions:

1. Peel pears, then cut them into eighths, discarding the cores.
2. Meanwhile, bring to a boil the grape juice, orange juice, vanilla, and brown sugar.
3. In each prepared 1 quart jar, place 1 anise pod, 1 cinnamon stick, 2 cloves, and 2 peppercorns.
4. Pack the jars with pear sections, leaving ½ inch of headspace.
5. Ladle the syrup over the pears and remove any air pockets.
6. Lid the jars and process in a water bath canner for 20-25-30 minutes, based on your altitude.

Merlot Spiced Pears

This is the be-all and end-all canned pear recipe. Not only does it taste decadent, but the way your house smells when you make it will bring everyone to the kitchen just to inhale it.

Ingredients:

- 2 bottles of merlot or other red wine (opt for a drier red than you would usually drink)
- 2 cups Turbinado (or white) sugar
- 1 cup water
- 2 tablespoons cinnamon powder
- 1 teaspoon clove powder

Directions:

1. Pour the wine and water into a saucepan and bring it to a simmer on low heat.
2. Meanwhile, mix the spices and sugar in a bowl until well combined.
3. When the wine mixture is simmering, stir in the sugar mixture. Stir with a whisk until the sugar and spices are dissolved in the wine.
4. Simmer on low heat for 15 minutes.
5. While the wine syrup is simmering, pack sliced pears into 6 sanitized quart jars.
6. Ladle the hot wine syrup over the pears, leaving 1/2 inch of headspace.
7. Process in a water bath canner for 20 minutes, adjusting for altitude.

Plain and Simple Pear Sauce

Another great way to use an abundance of pears is to make pear sauce. Slightly sweeter than apple sauce, it can be used in baking or substituted in any recipe in which you would normally use apple sauce.

I like to leave the skins on my pears since so many of the nutrients lurk there.

Ingredients:

- Pears
- Water as needed

Directions:

1. Wash the pears carefully using the method on page 237. If the pears are not organic, this will help to remove the pesticides in the event they have been sprayed.
2. Remove the cores and any dark spots.
3. Using a blender or food processer, puree the pears on a high setting.

4. Pour them into sanitized jars.
5. Process in a water bath canner for 20 minutes, adjusting for altitude.

Note: Pear sauce sometimes separates during the canning process. Don't be alarmed - it won't affect the quality or the taste. Simply shake the jar well before serving. Pear sauce is generally "thinner" in consistency than apple sauce, so use the smallest amount of water possible.

Just Peachy Peach Slices

A bushel of peaches will give you 20-24 quarts of peach slices to enjoy over the long winter. They are like bites of sunshine. Select freestone peaches – this will make your life far easier as they give up the pit without the vast effort required to remove the pit from clingstone peaches.

Peaches can be peeled just like tomatoes – dip them in boiling water for about a minute, then dunk them in ice water – the skin will almost get up and walk off by itself. (Okay, I confess, you'll have to help it a little.) The following recipe has no added sugar – my reason for preserving my own food is to provide healthier goodies for my family, so I use juice for canning whenever possible. You can follow the same procedure with a simple syrup if you prefer.

Ingredients:
- 1 bushel peeled freestone peaches
- 12 cups white grape juice
- 12 cups water
- 24 cinnamon sticks (optional)
- Bowl of lemon juice

Directions:

1. In a stockpot, bring white grape juice and water to a boil.
2. Cut peeled peaches in half, then slice them.
3. Immediately dip slices in lemon juice and then place them in a bowl.
4. Once your peaches are sliced, gently pour them into the juice/water mixture, taking care not to splash the boiling water on yourself.
5. Add a cinnamon stick to each jar if you have chosen to do so. (We usually put cinnamon in half the jars and leave the other half of the jars without.)
6. Ladle the peaches and liquid into the quart jars, leaving ½ inch of headspace.
7. Using a thin utensil like a table knife, remove any air pockets in the jars.
8. Lid your jars.
9. Peaches can be processed either in a water bath canner for 30-35-40 minutes, **OR** in a pressure canner for 10 minutes at 5-7 pounds of pressure. (I prefer the pressure canner because I feel more vitamins are preserved in the shorter cooking time.)

Plum Easy Plums

The easiest thing about this plum recipe is that there is virtually NO WORK unless you choose to add the step of slicing the plums in half and removing the stone at the time of processing. (You will end up with a mushier plum this way, but a thicker sauce.) And, to make matters even better, you end up with a delicious plummy sauce at the end!

Ingredients:

- 14 pounds small plums
- 7 cups white grape juice or apple juice
- 7 cups water

Directions:

1. Wash plums to remove pesticide, using the method on page 237.
2. If you are slicing the plums, cut them in half and remove the stone. If you are preserving them hole, using a fork, poke the plums at each end – otherwise you will have little exploding plums in your jars when processing.
3. Pack your jars with whole or halved plums.
4. Meanwhile, on the stove, bring to a boil your mixture of juice and water.
5. Ladle the hot liquid over the raw packed plums in quart jars.
6. Lid the jars.
7. You have two options for processing:
   ❖ In a water bath canner, process your jars for 25-30-35 minutes, based on altitude, **OR**
   ❖ In a pressure canner, process for 1- minutes at 5-7 pounds, based on altitude.

Tutti-Frutti Mixed Jars

Warning: Once you've tried this homemade fruit cocktail, you'll never be able to choke down that nasty, syrup-y stuff from the store again. Your family will insist that you make this every year! The mint adds a hint of fresh summery flavor to every jar, but is entirely optional.

This is a wonderful, whatever you have on hand kind of recipe – the proportions don't matter – go with whatever is cheap and abundant for you. For this reason, there are no measurements with this recipe – it will be different every time.

Ingredients:

- Peaches
- Pears
- Apples
- Plums
- Grapes
- Nectarines
- Apricots
- Cherries (pitted)
- A bowl of lemon juice
- Fresh mint (optional)

Liquid:

- 1:1 white grape or apple juice to water

Directions:

1. Wash all fruit using the pesticide-removing method outlined on page 237.
2. Cut fruit into bite sized pieces and dip the pieces in lemon juice, then place them into jars, evenly dispersing the different types of fruit across your batch.
3. Fill a stock pot with juice/water mixture.
4. Bring the entire concoction to a boil and then ladle it over the fruit into your ready-and-waiting sanitized quart jars.
5. Add a sprig of mint to each jar, lid the jars, and process in a water bath canner for 20 minutes, adjusting for altitude.

Very Very Orange Cherries

Ingredients:

- 10 pounds sweet cherries
- 3 cups red grape juice
- 1 cup orange juice
- 4 cups water

Directions:

1. Using a cherry pitter (less than a $10 investment that will literally save you hours!), remove the pits from the cherries and place them in quart jars, leaving ½ inch of head space.
2. Meanwhile, in a stockpot, heat the juices and water until boiling

3. Ladle the hot liquid into the jars, then remove any air pockets with a table knife run around the inside of the jar.
4. Lid the jars and process them in a p-canner for 10 minutes at 5 pounds of pressure.

NOTE: If you do not have a pressure canner, add the cherries to the boiling juice and cook for 10 minutes before placing them in the jars. Then process them in a water bath canner for 20 minutes, adjusting altitude.)

Bring on the Berries

Berries are among the easiest fruits to can because they require practically NO prep work and are actually best when a raw pack canning method is used.

This method works well with any berry that I have tried: blueberries, blackberries, raspberries, huckleberries, and strawberries have all been successful. You can also mix your berries for even more yumminess!

Ingredients:

- Berries (just under 2 pints per each 1 quart jar)
- 2 tablespoons lemon juice per quart jar
- Red or white grape juice and water at a 1:1 ratio

Directions:

1. Clean berries carefully by using the pesticide removal instructions found on page 237.
2. Place 2 tablespoons of lemon juice into each quart jar, than add in the berries, leaving ½ inch of headspace.

3. Meanwhile, bring your juice and water mixture to a boil in a large stock pot.
4. Lid the jars, then gently turn or shake them to remove air pockets from the bottom of the jar.
5. Remove the lids and ladle the hot liquid into the jars, allowing a minimum of ¼ inch of headspace. Wipe the lips of the jars carefully before re-capping them.
6. Berries can be processed two ways:

❖ Process your berries in a hot water bath canner for 20-25-30 minutes, based on altitude.
❖ Process your berries in a pressure canner at 5 pounds of pressure for 10 minutes.

❧ Venerable Vegetables ❦

Ahh...vegetables. They are the reason I began gardening in the first place, and, in response to that, canning. My yearning for year-round, affordable, organic, non-GMO produce provided the jumping off point for my two favorite hobbies.

We eat lots of vegetables. I would be hard-pressed to afford to buy them all at the natural food store. The perfect solution for summer is to raise my own veggies or hit up the farmer's market. But of course, we want vegetables in the winter too.

Taking it one step further, from a self-sufficiency standpoint, there may come a time when you will only eat what you can grow and preserve. Learning the best ways to store your garden bounty for the cold days ahead is vital.

Most of the vegetables here are canned simply, with very little seasoning. It's not that we dislike flavor, but if there is less seasoning in the jar, you can cook them up however you want them in the winter. I use the raw pack method whenever possible because, well, actually . . . because I'm lazy. Running a close second to my laziness is that the texture of veggies that have been cooked, then canned, is very mushy.

If you are using salt, place the desired amount in the bottom of your sanitized canning jars. When you pour water over the contents, the salt will disperse. Our preference is 1/8 teaspoon in pint jars and ¼ teaspoon in quart jars.

****Hint**: Take advantage of the vitamins stored in the liquid by using it for cooking grains like rice or barley, or adding it to soup stock. Vegetables contain very little acid. Therefore vegetables MUST be processed in a pressure canner. There is no gray area here, because the failure to do so can put you at risk for botulism.

Let me repeat the information on botulism from Chapter 1.

Botulism is a potentially lethal type of food poisoning that can grow in a low acid, low oxygen environment – I.E. – in your canned goods. **If it doesn't kill you, it can cause permanent paralysis or nerve damage.**

No one wants to serve that up to their families. A water bath canner does not reach and maintain a high enough temperature to kill off the bacteria that causes botulism – a pressure canner does.

I get emails all the time from people who tell me that their grandmother used a regular canner to preserve green beans and Grandma lived to the ripe old age of 99. My granny did too. People didn't put their children in car seats as recently as 30 years ago – most kids survived but there were a few that went bulleting through the front windshield.

We now possess the capability to make things safer than did our ancestors. Think how awful you would feel if your spouse or child died or suffered permanent physical damage because of something you fed them, against standard advice. It's not worth the risk.

One more note – I recommend a non-iodized salt, like canning salt or sea salt, if you plan to add salt to your vegetables. Iodized salt can make the veggies turn ugly colors.

Some veggies have a less than pleasant mushy texture when canned. If you don't like the result of some of your canning projects, be creative and think of other ways to use them. Try pureeing them and adding them to soup or mashed potatoes, for example.

Awesome Asparagus

We have found home-canned asparagus to be unpleasantly mushy on its own. With this warning in mind, if you end up with a windfall of asparagus, you can make a delicious, springtime cream-of-asparagus soup from your home-canned spears.

Ingredients:

- 15 pounds fresh asparagus
- Salt (optional)
- Water as needed

Directions:

1. Wash your asparagus carefully and gently.
2. Cut the spears into the proper lengths to fit inside your jars, discarding the woody ends.
3. Set a large pot of water to boil.
4. If you are using salt, place the desired amount in the bottom of your sanitized canning jars.
5. Load up the jars with your asparagus spears, packing them in tightly.
6. Ladle or pour boiling water into the jars, allowing 1 inch of headspace.
7. Use a utensil to remove any air pockets, then top up the water if needed.
8. Lid the jars and process them in your p-canner for 30 minutes at 10 pounds of pressure (40 minutes if you're using quart jars). Remember to adjust for altitude.

Carrots with Honey

Carrots can be jarred in any of a wide variety of shapes: coins, spears, ruffles, large chunks, or even whole (if they fit in the jar!) Totally up to you. Don't make them too small or they will be mushy and gross. Unless, of course, you like mushy carrots, then, hack away.

This year I canned them whole and they turned out with a far better texture than previous years, when I cut them into various other shapes. The bigger the pieces are, the better the results are. A drizzle of honey in each jar intensifies the natural sweetness of the carrots.

Ingredients:

- 10 pounds carrots
- Salt (optional)
- Water as needed
- ½ teaspoon honey or Turbinado sugar per jar (optional)

Directions:

1. Wash your carrots, then peel and slice them as desired.
2. Set a large pot of water to boil.
3. If you are using salt, place the desired amount in the bottom of your sanitized canning jars.
4. Load up the jars with your carrot pieces, packing them in tightly.
5. Ladle or pour boiling water into the jars, allowing 1 inch of headspace.
6. Use a utensil to remove any air pockets, then top up the water if needed.
7. Lid the jars and process them in your p-canner for 25 minutes at 10 pounds of pressure (30 minutes if you're using quart jars).

Corn is Cool

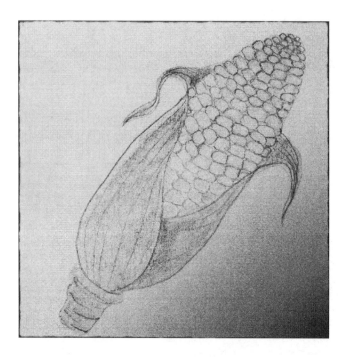

If you are fortunate enough to hit the mother lode of fresh, non-GMO corn, don't hesitate to put it into jars for delicious future consumption. There is quite honestly no comparison between this corn and the stuff you will get from grocery store tin cans.

Approximately 3 ears of corn will fill a pint jar when the kernels are removed from the cob.

Ingredients:

- Corn on the cob
- Salt (optional)
- Water as needed

Directions:

1. Husk the corn and remove the silk with a vegetable brush – this is a messy, back porch kind of job.
2. Slice the corn off the cob as closely as possible – it will come off in strips.

3. Fill your jars (I always use pints) with corn, leaving 1 inch of headspace. (Remember – corn expands in the p-canner – be sure you leave that inch!)
4. Ladle boiling water into the jars, allowing 1 inch of headspace.
5. Use a utensil to remove any air pockets, then top up the water if needed.
6. Lid the jars and process them in your p-canner for 55 minutes at 10 pounds of pressure (85 minutes if you're using quart jars).

Greenie Beanies

You can also use this process for wax beans or yellow beans, or (our favorite) a colorful combo of the three!

Ingredients:

- ½ bushel of green beans
- Salt (optional)
- Water as needed
- 1 clove garlic per jar (optional)

Directions:

1. Wash your beans carefully, then rinse them well.
2. Snap off the ends of your beans and then snap them into the desired size. Approximately 2 inch long pieces fit very nicely in the jars.

3. Set a large pot of water to boil.
4. If you are using salt, place the desired amount in the bottom of your sanitized canning jars.
5. Load up the jars with your beans, packing them in tightly.
6. Ladle or pour boiling water into the jars, allowing 1 inch of headspace.
7. Use a utensil to remove any air pockets, then top up the water if needed.
8. Lid the jars and process them in your p-canner for 20 minutes at 10 pounds of pressure (25 minutes if you're using quart jars).

Peas Please

These instructions are for any type of field peas – green peas, purple hull peas, black-eyed peas, or Crowder peas, for example. If you wish to can black-eyed peas with bacon, see the Hoppin' John recipe on page 205.

Ingredients:

- ½ bushel of peas
- Salt (optional)
- Water as needed

Directions:

1. Find a comfy place to sit with a couple of bowls, recruit some help, and start shelling peas.
2. Set a large pot of water to boil.
3. If you are using salt, place the desired amount in the bottom of your sanitized canning jars.
4. Load up the jars with your beans, packing them in tightly.

5. Ladle or pour boiling water into the jars, allowing 1 inch of headspace.
6. Use a utensil to remove any air pockets, then top up the water if needed.
7. Lid the jars and process them in your p-canner for 30 minutes at 10 pounds of pressure (40 minutes if you're using quart jars).

Perfect Pumpkin

It's common canning knowledge that you shouldn't can pumpkin and squash. However, it is actually just pumpkin and squash *purees* that should not be canned because the purees are so thick that they don't heat evenly, leaving them open to the risk of botulism. It's perfectly fine to can your pumpkin in chunks in a pressure canner, and then puree the pumpkin when you need it.

I leave my pumpkin totally without seasoning so that it can be used flexibly, in either sweet or savory dishes.

Ingredients:

- Uncooked pumpkin
- Boiling water as needed

Directions:

1. Cut up your pumpkin and remove the rind, seeds, and strings. (We always save the seeds for roasting.)
2. Cut the pumpkin into 1 inch chunks.
3. You can raw pack your pumpkin. Fill your quart jars with cubes, leaving 1 inch of headspace.
4. Fill the jar with hot water, keeping your inch of headspace.
5. Slide a utensil around the sides of the jar to remove air pockets.
6. Lid the jars and process them in your p-canner for 90 minutes at 11 pounds of pressure, adjusting for altitude.

Totally Tomatoes

I like to can some of my tomatoes as just plain and simple tomatoes. This is a little more versatile and I can use them in any type of recipe with any type of seasoning.

Because tomatoes are in actuality a fruit, not a vegetable, they are high acid enough to safely use a water bath canner. Instructions for both water bath canning and pressure canning are given.

Ingredients

- 20 pounds tomatoes
- 2 tablespoons lemon juice per jar
- Water as needed

Directions:

1. Prep your tomatoes as per the instructions on page 229.
2. Place your peeled, cored tomatoes in sanitized quart jars. You can cut them up or leave them whole.
3. Add 2 tablespoons of lemon juice to each jar.
4. Fill the jars with boiling water, leaving 1/2 inch of headspace.
5. Use a utensil to remove any air pockets - failure to do this could cause your jars not to seal.
6. Lid the jars.
7. If you're using a water bath canner, process the tomatoes for 45 minutes, adjusting for altitude.
8. If you're using a pressure canner, process the tomatoes for 15 minutes at 6 pounds of pressure, adjusting for altitude.

❧ Are You Nuts? ❧

f you are lucky enough to receive a windfall of nuts, whether from a tree n your backyard or a nearby forest, a great sale at the farmer's market, or a gift, you will want to make the most of it!

Sure, you could leave them in the bag you collected them in and store them in the freezer, but why not clear up that freezer space and prevent the possibility of loss or spoilage should a blackout occur?

Stick those babies in jars and you have something new to process in your water bath canner, as well as a shelf stable pantry treat!

When canning nuts, the water bath process is a little different. You do not want the water to cover the jars – you only need 2-3 inches of water in your canner, much like using a pressure canner.

Pecans

1. Shell your pecans, being careful to remove the bitter lining around the nut meat.
2. Spread your pecans on a baking sheet and place them in an oven that has been preheated to 325 degrees.
3. Bake the pecans only until heated through – you aren't trying to roast them – so for about 5 minutes.
4. Pour the hot nuts into dry, sanitized jars.
5. Place the lids on the jars.
6. Process the pecans in your water bath canner for 30 minutes, adjusting for your altitude.

Walnuts

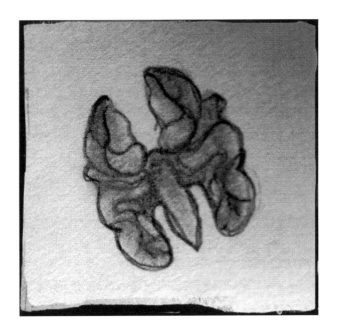

1. Shell your walnuts.
2. Spread the nuts on a baking sheet in a single layer.
3. Place the walnuts in the oven at 250 degrees. With walnuts, you are not roasting or cooking them – you are drying them out so that the oil does not become rancid. Stir them every 10 minutes so they don't get browned. This will take about 30 minutes.
4. Pack the hot nuts into dried, sanitized jars, allowing ½ inch of headspace.
5. Process them in your water bath canner for 30 minutes, adjusting for altitude.

Serving suggestion:

When it's time to open the jar and enjoy your walnuts, roast them at 275 for 20 minutes. Rub them to remove the skins before eating.

Hazelnuts

1. Shell your hazelnuts (also known as American Filberts).
2. Spread the nuts on a baking sheet in a single layer.
3. Place the hazelnuts in the oven at 250 degrees. As with walnuts, you are not roasting or cooking them – you are drying them out so that the oil does not become rancid. Stir them every 10 minutes so they don't get browned. This will take about 20 minutes.
4. Pack the hot nuts into dried, sanitized jars, allowing ½ inch of headspace.
5. Process them in your water bath canner for 30 minutes, adjusting for altitude.

Serving suggestion:

When it's time to open the jar and enjoy the hazelnuts, roast them at 275 for 20 minutes.

The
❧ Meat of the Matter ❧

This chapter is geared towards the "ingredients" of a meal, rather than a complete meal. Having a supply of already prepared basic meats on hand can go a long way towards speeding up mealtimes throughout the year. Canning meat is a great way to take advantage of a good sale or a bulk purchase without having to worry about what will happen if your freezer malfunctions or if you have a power outage.

The other benefit to canning your meat is that not only will it be preserved no matter what your electricity situation, it's immediately ready to eat. If you have a way to cook, you won't have to waste fuel actually cooking the meat. And worst case scenario, if you can't warm it up, it's safe to eat right out of the jar.

In a disaster situation, sufficient protein is extremely important. Without it, when you are performing hard manual labor, your body will begin to cannibalize your muscles to provide it with the nutrients – this will weaken you physically at a time when you need to be at your peak.

Meats **must** be canned using a pressure canner. (Remember our talks about botulism?) Most meat can be raw-packed – the heat of the canner will thoroughly cook the meat while it processes it.

About Roast Beast

Roast Beast applies to any type of roast that you might acquire: pork, beef, bison, venison, moose...you name it. When you hit the mother lode, whether it's a great sale, a successful hunt, or your side of beef has arrived, take some time to can it right away. Then you aren't subject to the whims of the electric grid and a great meal is as close as popping the lid off of a jar.

I like to plan for a full day of prep, canning, and clean-up when I have an abundance of meat in my freezer. This allows me to make the backbone of dozens of meals.

Tip: When canning meat, take special care when cleaning the lips of the jars – the fat content in meat can interfere in proper sealing if it gets between the jar and the lid. Try dipping a cloth or paper towel in white vinegar to break down any grease lingering on the lip of the jar.

Canning Prep

When dealing with a large amount of raw meat, I like to make it easy for myself. I cut open a cardboard box (which is how I get my groceries, so I have a free source of them) and lay it out on my freezer. Then I use a cookie sheet to hold the meat and place my cutting board in another cookie sheet. This way I don't have to clean up a bloody mess after preparing all that meat for canning. (I'm sure you know this but be certain to put a few drops of bleach in the wash water afterwards in order to kill bacteria left from the meat.)

I prefer to use wide-mouth jars for canning meat so that it isn't a wrestling match to get it out at serving time. When you pressure can the meat, it becomes fork tender, so you want to be able to remove it from the jar with a minimum of hassle.

First, slice the roasts into pieces that will fit into your sterilized jars. Then choose how you want to can it – following are two methods.

Raw Packed Roast Beast

Ingredients (per jar):

- 1 pound of roast (approximately)
- 1 clove garlic
- 2 small cooking onions, halved
- salt and pepper (optional)
- Water, as needed
- Optional - to make this a pot roast meal in a jar, feel free to add some carrot and potato chunks - there will be no change in the final processing times.

Directions:

1. Place a kettle of water on to boil.
2. Your jars should still be warm from being sterilized.
3. While waiting for the kettle to boil, place roast in each jar, leaving an inch and a half of space for the additional ingredients.
4. Add garlic, onions, salt, and pepper to each jar.
5. Pour water from the kettle into the jars over the meat and veggies. Using a table knife, run it down the sides of the jars to remove any air pockets, then top up if needed. Allow 1 inch of headspace.
6. Use a cloth with some vinegar on it to wipe the lip of the jars. If there is fat from the meat on the lip, the jars won't seal properly. Lid the jars.
7. Using your pressure canner, process the jars for 90 minutes at 10 pounds of pressure, adjusting for altitude.

Serving suggestion:

When you are ready to serve your roast, use the canning liquid to make gravy.

Barbecue Canned Beast

You may not want to can your entire beast as a simple roast – another great way to preserve your meat is in a homemade barbecue sauce. This sweet sauce is especially nice with game to reduce the flavor that some people find offensive. It can be used for either roast or for ground meat.

Ingredients for sauce:

- 6 cups crushed tomatoes (canned or fresh)
- 6 cloves garlic
- 3 small cooking onions
- 1/2 cup fresh bell pepper
- 1 cup brown sugar
- 1/4 cup white vinegar
- 1 teaspoon Worcestershire sauce
- 1 tablespoon hot sauce (like Frank's Red Hot) - optional
- 1/4 teaspoon powdered cloves
- 1 tablespoon paprika

Directions:

1. Using a food processor, puree peppers, garlic, and onion.
2. Mix all ingredients in a saucepan and bring to a boil.

3. Proceed with canning as for regular roast beast, above, replacing the water in the recipe with barbecue sauce. If you need more liquid, you can top up with water.

Serving suggestions:

At serving time, I like to shred the meat with two forks and stir it into the sauce before heating it up. Some separation of the sauce ingredients and the fat from the meat is perfectly normal. You can either discard the fat or stir it back in, depending upon your preference and dietary requirements.

Deep South BBQ

One more version of Roast Beast: This Southern classic can be made with any inexpensive roast, like beef or pork. The smoky flavorful meat only gets better as it sits in the jar.

Ingredients:

- 5-6 pound roast (an inexpensive cut is fine for this recipe)
- 1 bottle of beer

Sauce Ingredients:

- 2 cups ketchup
- ¼ cup prepared yellow mustard
- ½ cup brown sugar
- ¼ cup apple cider vinegar
- 1 tablespoon garlic powder
- 1 teaspoon black pepper
- 1 tablespoon liquid smoke
- ½ tablespoon Louisiana-style hot sauce

Directions:

1. Place the roast and onions in a slow cooker, then pour a bottle of beer over them.
2. Cook on low for 10 hours. The meat should be so delightfully tender that it falls apart when you touch it with a fork.
3. Shred the meat with two forks and return it to the cooking liquid in the crockpot. Stir it to combine.
4. In a saucepan, combine sauce ingredients with a whisk.
5. Stirring frequently, bring the sauce ingredients to a boil.
6. Pour the sauce over the meat in the crockpot. Stir well.
7. Heat on low in the crockpot for another 30 minutes.
8. Ladle the hot meat and sauce into sanitized jars. (Pint jars hold approximately 1 pound of cooked meat)
9. Lid the jars and process them in a p-canner for 70 minutes at 10 pounds of pressure. If you are using quart jars, process at the same pressure for 90 minutes.

Serving suggestions:

The meat can be served on a bun or just deliciously piled on a plate and paired with coleslaw.

Meximeat

For instant gratification of those fiesta cravings, preserve some ground meat that is already seasoned and ready to fill a tortilla. Going with the "use what you've got" principle, you can use ground beef, ground chicken, or ground whatever for these flavorful pints.

Reducing the amount of fat is not only better for your waistline, it's better for the preservation of your food. A high fat item is more vulnerable to spoilage. After precooking the meat, carefully drain the fat before adding the seasoning.

(**NOTE**: a pint jar holds about 1 pound meat.)

Ingredients:

- 5 pounds ground beef/ground whatever
- 2 large onions, finely minced
- 6 cloves garlic, finely minced
- 1 tablespoon olive oil
- 2 cans tomato paste
- ½ cup chili powder
- ¼ cup cumin powder

Directions:

1. Using a food processor, mince the onion and garlic finely.
2. Add olive oil to a large stock pot and lightly sauté the onion and garlic.
3. Add your ground meat to the pot, stirring well to combine it with the onion and garlic.
4. Pour in enough water to cover the meat/veggie mixture.
5. Bring the contents of the stockpot to a boil, then reduce heat until the mixture is simmering lightly. Cook for about 1 hour, stirring occasionally.
6. Using a metal colander, drain your meat mixture carefully. (If you really want your product to be lean, you can also rinse the meat under running water – I usually skip that step.)
7. Return the meat and veggie mixture to the stockpot and stir well to combine the tomato paste and spices.
8. Immediately ladle the mixture into prepared 1 pint jars, leaving 1/2 inch of headspace.
9. Process the jars in a p-canner for 75 minutes at 10 pounds of pressure, adjusting for altitude.

Serving suggestions:

Use this meat anywhere you'd use freshly cooked taco filling: on nachos, topping a taco salad, filling a tortilla...the list is endless!

Sloppy Joe Filling

Some things taste better than they look, and this filling is one of those things. It's absolutely delicious, but once it cools in the jars, there is some separation.

Don't be deterred by the lengthy prep time – very little of it is hands-on time. As well, you can reserve some Sloppy Joe meat for dinner instead o canning the entire batch.

Ingredients:

- 6 pounds prepped tomatoes (page 229)
- 2 cups chopped onions
- 2 cups chopped sweet bell peppers
- 2 cloves garlic, minced
- 1 ½ cups brown sugar
- 2 tablespoons smoked or regular paprika
- salt and pepper to taste
- 1/2 cup apple cider vinegar
- 5 pounds lean ground beef or turkey

Directions:

1. Using a food processor, puree the tomatoes, bell peppers, and garlic in batches.
2. Pour the vegetable puree into your crockpot and cook it on low for about 6-8 hours with the lid askew. The volume should be reduced by half.
3. Stir in the sugar, spices, and vinegar and continue to cook on low until the mixture has reached the desired consistency (2-4 more hours).
4. On a stove top, lightly brown ground beef and drain in a metal colander.
5. Stir the drained beef into the sauce.
6. Ladle the sauce into sanitized pint jars – this will fill approximately 6-7 jars.
7. Wipe the lips of the jars, then place the lids on.
8. Process in a p-canner for 90 minutes at 10 pounds of pressure.

Serving suggestions:

Remember, you may notice a bit of grease separated in your jar of sauce and meat. This is not unusual. You can either drain it off before reheating or stir it in. Once you've reheated your sauce, serve it on a bun or pita for a classic Sloppy Joe. Add a side of coleslaw!

Skinless Boneless Chicken

Raw-packing skinless boneless chicken results in a delicious, tender poached chicken that is delicious cut up into chicken salads or shredded and seasoned to be used in enchiladas or other chicken-containing recipes. For the sake of versatility, this recipe contains only very mild seasoning.

Each quart jar will hold approximately 3 average sized chicken breasts or 6 chicken thighs. The following recipe is *per jar* – multiply the ingredients as needed.

Ingredients:

- 3 skinless boneless chicken breasts or 6 skinless boneless thighs
- 1 clove crushed garlic
- ½ teaspoon sea salt
- ½ teaspoon black pepper
- Water as needed

Directions:

1. Place one clove of garlic in the bottom of each sanitized quart jar.
2. Add raw chicken pieces to the jar, pushing them down to pack tightly.
3. Add salt and pepper, and then top up the jar with water, allowing 1 inch of headspace.
4. IMPORTANT: Skipping this step may cause your jars not to seal. Carefully slide a table knife or other narrow utensil down the interior sides of the jars, removing air pockets.
5. Lid the jars and process in a pressure canner for an hour and a half at 10 pounds of pressure, adjusting for altitude.

❧ Making the Most of Leftovers ❦

It's that time of year: your refrigerator is stuffed to the point that you have to lean against the door to close it and you never want to see another bite of turkey, ham, or roast beef again.

So what can a thrifty person do with all of that delicious bounty?

Preserve it!

An added bonus to the Thanksgiving holiday feast is the boon that it can give to your pantry. If you have some jars and fresh lids, your kitchen already contains everything you need to add an abundant amount of food to your pantry.

Nearly all of your post-holiday goodies can be put back for future use, adding to your shelves full of home-preserved ingredients. Don't let anything go to waste. Many people wait too long to preserve the food and end up having to throw most of it in the trash.

Turkey, veggies, and cranberry sauce will all make beautiful additions to your home-canned goods. Use these recipes as a guideline to adapt what you have left over to nutritious homemade meals in jars.

Make it a tradition to spend a day in the kitchen once the holidays are over and put away that food for later!

Leftover Roast Beast

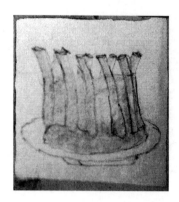

This is a great way to preserve virtually any roast that you have in abundance – beef, bison, venison, or pork, for example.

Ingredients:

- Cooked roast
- Onion, quartered
- 1 clove garlic per jar, crushed
- Broth, red wine, or water to top off each jar
- Other spices according to personal tastes (peppercorns, paprika, chili powder, etc.) – be certain to use a light hand with spices, as they will intensify when canned

Directions:

1. Cook your roast as per your usual method or recipe.
2. When it's cool, take the section you intend to preserve and slice it thinly.
3. In the bottom of each jar, place your clove of crushed garlic and a wedge of onion, as well as any spices you intend to use.
4. Place the slices of beast vertically into the jars, packing the jar loosely.
5. Top the meat with the appropriate broth, based on the type of meat you are using. You can also use water for your canning liquid. Allow 1 inch of headspace.
6. Process the meat for 75 minutes in a pressure canner at 10 pounds.

Note: Do not add flour to the broth for "gravy" - it doesn't store well. Instead, make fresh gravy from the broth when you open the jar.

Home Canned Ham How-To

In a totally different stratosphere from Spam, the cans of flaked ham, and the big pear-shaped cans of ham in some mysterious congealed substance that you get from the grocery store, is home-canned ham.

Every Christmas I get a spiral-cut, naturally cured ham. It is pricy, but very delicious. I bake it in a nice orange-brown sugar glaze and we pick away at it for a few days. Always reserve your cooking liquid in the refrigerator to use when you're canning.

Then, in order to get our money's worth, I spend several hours canning the abundant leftovers.

It's important to note that home canned ham gets incredibly salty as it sits in the jar. It doesn't work well as a stand-alone meat but it's a delicious addition to casseroles, beans, soups, or scalloped potatoes. Because of this, I prefer to can ham in pint jars instead of quart jars.

Directions:

1. Begin with your rather motley looking piece of ham on the bone.
2. Using a sharp knife, remove as much ham as possible from the bone.
3. Meanwhile, be bringing your reserved cooking liquid to a boil on the stove. You may want to add 2 cups of water to thin it down to a broth-like consistency.
4. Place the pieces into sanitized jars.
5. (You will have some fattier pieces that you won't want to eat - put those aside for the broth you're going to make.)
6. Fill pint jars with ham pieces.
7. Ladle the hot broth in, leaving 1 inch of headspace. If you don't have broth, you can use water or chicken broth for this.
8. Wipe the lip of the jar with a cloth dipped in vinegar and lid the jars. Pressure can pints for 75 minutes for at 10 PSI, adjusting for altitude. (Process 90 minutes for quarts)

Making Ham Broth

Don't stop at simply canning the meat – now it's time to make broth. This broth can be used as a soup base, for cooking grains like rice, or in any recipe requiring liquid in which the smoky flavor of ham would be tasty. I like to use my slow cooker to make broth, but this can also be simmered all day long on the stovetop. Caution: don't add salt – it will be far too strong if you do.

Ingredients:

- Hambone and leftover meat
- 1 onion, quartered
- 2-6 cloves garlic, smashed
- Bay leaf
- 2 carrots, peeled
- Enough water to fill the crockpot

Directions:

1. Place the ham bone and any unappetizing pieces of meat into your crockpot.
2. Add onion, garlic, carrots, and bay leaf.
3. Cover the contents of the crockpot with water and fill to the top.
4. Place the lid on and then cook on low for 10 hours.
5. Use a metal colander to strain the broth.
6. Use it immediately or can the broth.

Canning Directions:

1. Ladle the hot strained broth into quart jars, leaving 1 inch of headspace.
2. Wipe the lip of the jar with a cloth dipped in vinegar and lid the jars.
3. Pressure can for 90 minutes at 10 PSI, adjusting for altitude.

Sugar Baked Ham

Directions are "per jar" – this is a great way to put away those endless leftovers after Christmas or Easter dinner! I use pint jars for canning ham. This sweeter ham is a yummy addition to baked beans or any other dish that is sweet-savory.

Ingredients:

- 4 ½-inch thick slices of ham
- 3 tablespoons brown sugar
- 1 teaspoon grainy prepared mustard
- 1 teaspoon apple cider vinegar
- 4 whole cloves

Directions:

1. Make a paste of the mustard, sugar, and vinegar, and spread it on one side of the ham.
2. Roll each slice and insert them into the jar.
3. Top each ham roll with a clove.
4. Do not add liquid.
5. Clean off the lip of the jar and cap them with snap lids and rings.
6. Process the ham in a pressure cooker for 40 minutes at 10 pounds.

What can you do with home-canned ham?

- As mentioned, the flavor of the ham becomes much more intense as it sits in the jar. Be careful about adding salt when you open the jar and add the ham to another food you are preparing.
- The ham pieces can be sautéed and added to scrambled eggs or in place of bacon to top baked potatoes or soup.
- The ham and broth can be used to make red-eye gravy.
- The ham pieces can also be used in casseroles and scalloped potatoes.
- The broth is a delicious base for soups, cooking rice or wheat berries, or for cooking beans or other legumes.

Shredded Turkey

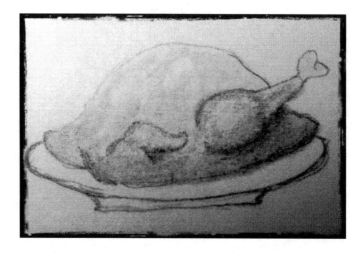

If you have lots of turkey left, you can shred the meat with two forks and then jar it up for use in recipes like enchiladas, soft tacos, casseroles, or drenched in barbecue sauce for sandwiches. (Cooked chicken can be preserved using the same instructions.)

Ingredients (listed per jar):

- Roasted turkey, shredded
- 1 clove of crushed garlic
- ¼ of an onion
- ¼ teaspoon sea salt
- ½ teaspoon black pepper (or to taste)
- Water as needed

Directions:

1. Place garlic and onion in the bottom of jars.
2. Fill the jars with shredded turkey, topping off with salt and pepper.
3. Pour hot water over the contents of the jars.
4. **IMPORTANT**: Skipping this step may cause your jars not to seal. Carefully slide a table knife or other narrow utensil down the interior sides of the jars, removing air pockets.
5. Lid the jars and process in a p-canner for 90 minutes for quarts or 75 minutes for pints at 13 pounds of pressure, adjusting for altitude.

Making Turkey Stock

After a few meals of roasted turkey, remove most of the meat from the bones and place it in the refrigerator.

You'll be left with a rather desolate-looking carcass, but don't be deterred. This is canning GOLD! Be sure and check your holiday veggie tray for vegetables that can be added to the cooking pot. **An important note about spices**: Sage tastes horrible when canned – if it is normally an ingredient in your chicken soup, add it at the time that you heat and serve it.

Ingredients:

- Carcass, giblets, neck, and lower quality meat
- Assorted uncooked vegetable: carrots, peppers
- 1 head of garlic
- 2-4 onions (Note: there's no need to peel the garlic and onions as long as they are organic - just wash them well.)
- 2 tablespoons salt
- Spices of choice: try whole peppercorns, salt, oregano, basil, and/or bay leaves

Directions for stock:

1. Place all ingredients in the crockpot.
2. Fill the crockpot right to the top with water.
3. Put the crockpot on low for 12-14 hours and let it simmer undisturbed overnight... *Zzzzzzzz......*
4. The next day, strain the contents of the crockpot into a large container - I use a big soup pot and a metal colander.
5. Allow the bones to cool, then remove any meat that you would like to add to your soup.

I always give our dog a big treat - a bowl of turkey with gristle, fat, and skin. She's a little on the skinny side because she runs constantly when she's outside so I think that the occasional fat intake is good for her. She also likes the mushy carrots. I usually divide the "sludge" into a few different servings of treats for her.

Directions for canning:

1. Take all of the meat that you put in the refrigerator the night before and cut it into bite-sized pieces. I like a mixture of light meat and dark meat for this purpose.
2. Also cut up the meat you removed from the crockpot.
3. Place approximately 1 cup of turkey in each of your sanitized jars. (Give or take a little!)
4. Add 1-2 cloves of garlic to the jars.
5. You will have a rich, dark, beautiful stock from the overnight crockpot project. Ladle this over your cut-up turkey and garlic, leaving 1 inch of headspace at the top of the jars. (If you run out of broth, top it up with water - your broth will still be very flavorful.)
6. Wipe the lip of your jars with a cloth dipped in white vinegar.
7. Place the lids on and process them in your p-canner for 90 minutes at 10 pounds, adjusting for altitude.

These deep golden, rich meaty jars are an excellent base for turkey and dumplings, as well as any type of turkey soup.

Canning Cranberry Sauce

If you have leftover cranberry sauce, you may can it for future use. I like to use teeny little half pint jam jars for this.

1. Heat the cranberry sauce to a simmer on the stovetop.
2. Ladle the sauce into sanitized jars, leaving 1/4 inch of headspace.
3. Wipe the rims of the jars, then place the lid on them.
4. Process in a water bath canner for 15 minutes, adjusting for altitude.

Thanksgiving Soup

The ultimate leftover canning concoction has to be the eclectic "Thanksgiving Soup". An example I made one year contained carrots that were cooked in honey, green beans with some butter, some diced sweet potatoes, and corn with butter.

Ingredients:

- Round up whatever veggies that you have left over from Thanksgiving. (Don't worry if they have some butter and seasonings on them - it will all add to the rich flavor of your soup.)
- Raid your veggie tray: chop your crudités into bite sized pieces and add them raw to your jars - they'll cook beautifully during the canning process.
- 1 cup diced turkey per jar
- 1 clove garlic per jar
- 2 tablespoons chopped onion per jar
- 1 cup of stock per jar
- Diced potatoes (optional)
- Water as needed

Directions:

1. Place your leftovers, potatoes, and chopped crudités into a large bowl and combine them well.
2. Add one cup of your vegetable mixture to each sanitized quart jar.
3. Add 1 cup of chopped turkey to each jar.
4. Season with a clove of garlic and 1-2 tablespoons of chopped onion in each jar
5. Top your veggies and turkey with one cup of the delicious stock that you made from the turkey carcass.
6. Fill the jar the rest of the way with water. The flavors will blend - don't worry!
7. Wipe the lip of your jars with a cloth dipped in white vinegar and then place the lids on.
8. Process the soup in your pressure canner for 90 minutes at 10 pounds of pressure, adjusting for altitude.

Variations:

- If you want a different type of soup, add 2 tablespoons of tomato paste to each jar and season with some Italian spices like basil and oregano.
- At serving time, you can add some cooked rice, barley, or pasta to your soup.

❧ Meals in Jars ❧

These main dishes require only quick side dishes to allow you to have a great meal on the table faster than you can say "drive-thru". The simple addition of a grain like brown rice, quinoa, or pasta and perhaps a vegetable or salad on the side (depending on availability and season) will make it seem like you slaved all afternoon over a hot stove as opposed to just opening a jar and boiling some water.

A few of the meals, like Stroganoff, would be enhanced by stirring in some sour cream at serving time. See the "Serving Suggestions" at the end of each recipe.

All ingredients are uncooked unless the recipe specifically states otherwise. This protects vegetables from being mushy and overcooked, and pressure cooks the meat to create a flavorful broth and provide a fork tender result.

Hungarian Goulash

Goulash is generally served over spaetzle, egg noodles, rice, or mashed potatoes.

Ingredients:

- 4 pounds of stewing meat (beef, pork, etc.)
- 4 tablespoons REAL Hungarian paprika (it must be the real stuff for an authentic flavor)
- 2 teaspoons dry mustard
- Salt and pepper to taste
- 4 onions, quartered
- 4 cloves minced garlic
- 1 tablespoon olive oil
- 4 carrots, sliced into large pieces
- 6 potatoes, diced
- 2 bell peppers, diced
- 1 can of tomato paste
- ½ cup red wine vinegar
- Water as needed

Directions:

1. In a bowl, mix Hungarian paprika, dry mustard, salt, and pepper.

2. In a large stockpot, heat olive oil and begin to sauté your onions and garlic.
3. Dip your stewing meat in the spice mixture, then place the meat in the stockpot to brown with the garlic and onions. You only need to brown lightly – the meat doesn't need to be cooked.
4. In quart jars, layer your meat and vegetable mixture, carrots, peppers, and potatoes.
5. Add 6 cups of water, vinegar, and tomato paste to the stock pot and mix with any drippings or spices that remain after browning the meat. Bring this mixture to a boil.
6. Ladle hot liquid into jars over the layered contents. Use a table knife to remove any air pockets in the jars. If necessary, top up with water, allowing 1 inch of headspace.
7. Lid the jars and process in your p-canner for one hour and 15 minutes at 10 pounds of pressure, based on altitude.

Serving suggestions:

When heating your goulash, whisk in 1 tablespoon of flour to thicken the sauce. Once it is hot, stir in a half cup of sour cream and heat only until the sour cream is warmed through.

Beef Stroganoff

Beef stroganoff is delicious served over egg noodles or rice.

Ingredients:

- 3-4 pounds stewing beef or sliced sirloin
- 2 onions, finely chopped
- cloves of garlic, finely chopped
- 4 cups mushrooms, sliced
- 1 tablespoon butter
- 2 tablespoons Worcestershire sauce
- Salt and pepper to taste
- Water to deglaze pan

Directions:

1. In a large stockpot, sauté beef, onions, garlic and mushrooms in butter until lightly browned.
2. Stir in Worcestershire sauce and enough water to deglaze the stockpot. Use a metal utensil to scrape the bottom of the pot to loosen the flavorful pieces there.
3. Add 1 cup of water and stir well, bringing to a boil.
4. Ladle the stroganoff into sanitized quart jars, distributing the sauce evenly across the jars
5. Process in your p-canner for 90 minutes at 10 pounds of pressure, adjusting for altitude.

Serving Suggestions:

When you are ready to serve the beef stroganoff, stir 1 cup of sour cream or plain yogurt into the heated sauce. Continue heating the sauce at a low temperature only until the addition is warmed through.

Cajun Jambalaya

The beautiful thing about jambalaya (aside from its incredible blend of Cajun flavors) is that it's one of those use-what-you've-got kinds of recipes: ham, chicken, sausage or even all three. At serving time you can toss in some fresh shrimp too.

This recipe won't look like the other "meal" recipes – it will look more like a soup. You need to cook rice in the flavorful broth at serving time. So use quart jars and make sure each one contains at least 2 cups of liquid.

Ingredients:

- 3-4 pounds boneless chicken thighs and breasts, cut into bite sized pieces
- 2 cups thinly sliced smoked sausage
- 2 cups chopped onion
- 2 cups chopped green and/or red bell pepper
- 2 ribs celery, chopped
- 6 cloves of garlic, minced
- 1 tablespoon olive oil
- 2 tablespoons each of smoked paprika, Cajun spice blend, and thyme
- Salt, cayenne, and black pepper to taste
- 1/4 teaspoon hot pepper sauce (Tabasco)
- 6 cups of peeled tomatoes with juice
- 4 cups each chicken broth and water

Directions:

1. In a large stockpot lightly brown the first 6 ingredients in olive oil.
2. In a small bowl, mix paprika, salt, pepper, thyme, cayenne, and Cajun spice blend.
3. Sprinkle the vegetable and meat mixture with spice mixture, then add tomatoes, and stir well to combine.
4. Ladle the ingredients into sanitized quart jars filling them no more than halfway.
5. Meanwhile, place the broth, tomato juice, and water in the stockpot and bring it to a boil, deglazing the bottom of the pot.
6. Ladle 2 cups of hot liquid into each jar, allowing 1 inch of headspace. You can top up with water if you need to.
7. Lid the jars and process in a pressure canner for an hour and a half at 10 pounds of pressure, adjusting for altitude.

Serving Suggestions:

When it's Jambalaya time, add 1 cup of rice to the contents of your jar. Bring it to a boil, reduce heat, put the lid on, and simmer until your rice is cooked and most or all of the liquid has been absorbed. Remove from heat and fluff rice. Allow the dish to sit for 5 minutes covered, then enjoy the rich Cajun flavor!

Chicken Cacciatore

The rich herbed tomato sauce and the tender chicken will not last long on the pantry shelves – as soon as you serve one jar of it, your family will beg you to make it again!

To make life even simpler, this is a raw-pack recipe!

Ingredients:

- 3 pounds boneless chicken, cut into bite sized pieces (a mix of breasts and thighs is nice)
- 2 cups red and green peppers, cut into chunks
- 2 cups onion, cut into 8ths
- 2 cups mushrooms, sliced
- cloves of garlic
- 4 cups diced tomatoes, with juice
- 1 bottle of red wine
- 2 tablespoons oregano
- 2 tablespoons basil
- 2 tablespoons thyme
- Salt and pepper to taste

Directions:

1. Layer chicken, peppers, onions, mushrooms, and garlic in quart jars.
2. In a large stockpot bring wine, tomatoes, and herbs to a boil.
3. Ladle hot liquid over the layered ingredients in your jars.
4. Lid the jars and process them in your p-canner for 90 minutes at 11 pounds of pressure, based on altitude.

Serving Suggestions:

When preparing the cacciatore, stir in a small can of tomato paste when heating it to thicken the sauce. Serve over pasta or rice, with a side of garlic bread.

Snowfall Spaghetti Sauce

The rule in our house is that you don't open the spaghetti sauce until the first snow. My little one always eagerly awaits the first flake and runs home to tell me, "We're having spaghetti! It's snowing!"

The reason we wait to open the sauce is because it gets better when it sits for a few months. The depth of flavor combined with the freshness of the ingredients makes this a hit. I make enough sauce for spaghetti twice a month.

There is a variation at the end of the recipe where you can add ground meat or meatballs to this classic marinara sauce.

Following is the step by step for making and canning your own Italian marinara sauce. It's easy, healthy, and delicious, and a great way to make use of a bounty of tomatoes.

Homemade marinara sauce is a world away from the stuff you buy in the grocery store. It's loaded with vitamins and nutrients, and not tainted by BPA, additives, and high fructose corn syrup.

Don't be put off by the hands-on time needed to make this. Consider that if you made 14 from-scratch spaghetti dinners, it would take you far more time than the six hours that these two batches of sauce took.

It takes approximately 1 pound of tomatoes to make 1 quart jar of sauce. The following instructions are for a canner load full of sauce or 7 quarts.

1. Prep 7 pounds of tomatoes as per the instructions on page 229.
2. Using a food processor or blender, puree 2 bell peppers, 2 large onions, and 1 or 2 heads of garlic.
3. Add the prepped tomatoes and veggies to a large stockpot.
4. Then add the following seasonings - the first amount is per pound of tomatoes, and the second amount is for a 7 quart batch of sauce.

   - 1 tablespoon - **sugar** - 1/3 cup
   - 1 teaspoon - **sea salt** - 2 and 1/2 tablespoons
   - 1 teaspoon - **thyme** - 2 and 1/2 tablespoons
   - 1 tablespoon - **oregano** - 1/3 cup
   - 1 tablespoon - **basil** - 1/3 cup
   - 1 pinch - **powdered clove (trust me!)** - 1 tablespoon
   - **black pepper to taste**
   - 1 pinch - **paprika (smoked Hungarian if you can find it)** - 1 tablespoon
   - 2 tablespoons - **extra virgin olive oil** - 2/3 cup

5. With the lid on, bring the sauce to a simmer for about an hour, stirring occasionally. Then, remove the lid, drop the heat and simmer gently for 3 more hours. Removing the lid will allow the liquid to evaporate so that the sauce can cook down and thicken.

Canning Directions:

When it's time to can the sauce, don't worry if the consistency is still a little bit watery. Over its time on the shelf, it will thicken a little bit. If at serving time it is still runnier than you prefer, simply stir in a small tin o tomato paste to thicken it.

1. Fill sanitized quart jars with sauce, allowing 1 inch of headspace.
2. Wipe the lip of your jars with a cloth dipped in white vinegar and then place the lids on.
3. Process the sauce in your pressure canner for 25 minutes at 7 pounds of pressure, adjusting for altitude.
4. Allow the jars to cool undisturbed for at least 12 hours or until cooled. Test the seals before putting them away.

Now you have many quarts of delicious, authentic Italian marinara sauce to serve at pasta dinners to come. You can use this to make spaghetti and meatballs, chicken parmesan, as the base of an Italian vegetable soup, or you can thicken it to use as a pizza sauce.

Mangia bene!

(Eat well!)

Meanwhile, you can make meatballs...

Meatballs can very nicely. I have always made them eggless because my youngest daughter is allergic to eggs. It seems as though these slightly dry meatballs hold together better during the canning process than the ones that contain egg. You can use whatever type of ground meat you have on hand.

Meatball ingredients:

- 5 pounds ground beast
- 2 cups very fine crumbs (I freeze bread for this purpose and use a food processor to make the crumbs)
- 2 tablespoons salt (note: account for the salt in your source of crumbs and adjust accordingly)
- 2 tablespoons dried parsley flakes
- 1 tablespoon garlic powder
- 1 tablespoon onion powder

Canning Directions:

1. Combine all of the meatball ingredients in a large bowl, using your hands to mix well.
2. Form very firm meatballs. The right size fits nicely in the palm of your hand.
3. Place 8-10 meatballs into each sterilized quart jar - don't over fill the jars with meatballs because you want to leave room for sauce.
4. Cover the meatballs with hot marinara sauce.
5. Very gently use a spatula to remove air pockets so that the sauce completely fills the jar, allowing 1 inch of headspace at the top.
6. Process for 90 minutes in a p-canner at 10 pounds of pressure and adjusting for altitude.

Also you can do a batch with meat sauce...

Meat Sauce ingredients...

- 3-4 pounds ground meat (beef, pork, or whatever you have on hand)
- 1 tablespoon onion powder
- Salt and pepper to taste

Directions:

1. Brown the ground meat in a large skillet, stirring in seasonings.
2. Drain the meat and blot it with a paper towel to remove some of the fat.
3. Fill quart jars half way with meat, then ladle hot spaghetti sauce over the meat. Use a kitchen knife to remove air pockets and top up with more sauce.
4. Wipe the lip of the jar carefully, and put the lids on.
5. Process the meat sauce in your p-canner for 90 minutes at 10 pounds of pressure, adjusting for altitude.

Beans, Beans, Good for Your...

Beans are a pantry staple for many people, but they sure do take a long time to cook!

This is fine in normal circumstances - you just need to plan ahead, soak them, and let them simmer for a few hours.

However, in a down-grid situation, this can be easier said than done. I've cooked them on my woodstove before and it took an entire day, and required constant stoking of the fire to keep the heat up enough. It is going to use up far too much fuel to make a humble pot of beans.

For this reason, I always have some jars of home canned beans on my shelves. There's a lot of room for variety when home-canning your beans. You can use whatever beans you have on hand for this: navy beans, white kidney beans, black beans, pinto beans, or even a mix of a few different kinds. And finally, if you need to, feel free to leave out the meat. Some have religious restrictions or follow a vegetarian diet. Just skip the addition of the meat and carry on with the rest of the instructions.

When canning beans they must be soaked ahead of time, then the pressure canning process will do the rest of the work. The beans must be totally covered with liquid and there must be room for them to expand.

Some question the price efficiency of canning my own beans instead of buying pre-canned beans at the store. This is a valid point - they end up, with the price of power to can them and the use of a jar lid, to be about the same price as the conventional store-bought canned beans. But if you are using organic beans and comparing the home-canned to store bought organic beans, doing it yourself is far cheaper.

And...

- I know exactly what is in the beans I can myself - I am certain they contain no high-fructose corn syrup, no additives to maintain texture or appearance, and no hidden MSG.
- I'm assured of the quality of meat that I'm using. The pork in home canned pork and beans will be the pork you have selected, hopefully from a local farm that does not use growth hormones or antibiotics and where they don't feed their pigs GMO feed. I know the meat is not some congealed "meat by-product".
- I know the beans have been carefully washed and sorted by hand, not sifted through some machine that might not catch everything I would.

Yeah, I know - I'm picky! But once you taste these beans, you'll see why it's worth it to go the extra mile to make them!

Basic Pork and Beans

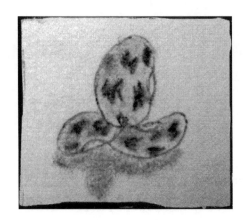

After the canning recipe, read on for some variations on the basic recipe. This recipe has worked on any type of bean I've tried it with, including pinto, navy, black, red kidney, white kidney, chick peas (garbanzos), and black-eyed peas. Adjust the meat you add according to what will blend nicely with your bean of choice, as well as how you intend to use the beans in the future. There are two variations at the end of the recipe.

NOTE: I tried this once without pre-soaking the beans and the results were poor. The beans had to be further cooked in liquid when I opened the jar. They soaked up all the liquid and were not fully cooked. This was resolved by two different methods: adding them to soup and letting them cook for another hour or two when I opened the jar, or making oven-baked beans.

Ingredients:

- 3 pounds dried beans
- 1-2 pounds ham, salt pork or bacon
- salt (optional)
- 6 small onions, cut in half
- 12 bay leaves
- water or broth as needed

Directions:

1. Rinse and sort dried beans, then soak them in hot water for at least 2 hours.
2. Discard the soaking water, then bring to a boil in fresh water or broth.
3. Drain the beans again, this time reserving the cooking water.
4. Distribute the pork evenly across sanitized pint jars.
5. Top the meat with soaked beans, filling each jar no more than 2/3 full.
6. Add to each jar a pinch of salt, 2 bay leaves and an onion.
7. In the bean pot, bring 6 cups of the reserved liquid (topping up with water to get to the proper amount if necessary) to a boil.
8. Ladle the hot liquid over the beans, leaving 1-1/2 inches of headspace. The beans must be totally covered with liquid and there must be room for them to expand.
9. Lid the jars and process in a pressure canner for 75 minutes for pints, 90 minutes for quarts, at 10 pounds of pressure, adjusting for altitude.

Mexican Pork and Beans

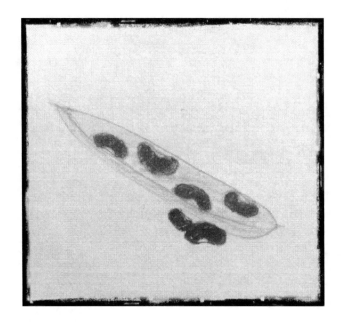

Ingredients:

- 3 pounds dried black beans or pinto beans
- 1-2 pounds salt pork or bacon
- salt (optional)
- boiling water as needed

Per jar:

- ¼ teaspoon garlic powder
- ¼ teaspoon onion powder
- ¼ teaspoon chili powder
- 1/8 teaspoon cumin
- 1 tablespoon tomato paste
- ½ onion

Directions:

1. Rinse and sort dried beans, then soak them in hot water for at least 2 hours.
2. Discard the soaking water, then bring to a boil in fresh water or broth.
3. Drain the beans again, this time reserving the cooking water.
4. Distribute the pork evenly across sanitized pint jars.
5. Top the meat with soaked beans, filling each jar no more than 2/3 full.
6. Add to each jar a pinch of salt, garlic powder, onion powder, cumin, chili powder, tomato paste, and an onion.
7. In the bean pot, bring 6 cups of the reserved liquid (topping up with water to get to the proper amount if necessary) to a boil.
8. Ladle the hot liquid over the beans, leaving 1-1/2 inches of headspace. The beans must be totally covered with liquid and there must be room for them to expand.
9. Lid the jars and process in a pressure canner for 75 minutes for pints, 90 minutes for quarts, at 10 pounds of pressure, adjusting for altitude.

Serving suggestions:

These are yummy popped right into a tortilla for bean burritos or heated and mashed slightly to make "refried beans".

BBQ Beans

These are your basic Southern picnic beans, delicious served warm, cold or at room temperature.

Ingredients:

- 3 pounds navy, kidney, cannellini, or pinto beans
- 1-2 pounds salt pork, ham, or bacon
- salt (optional)
- 6 cups tomato juice
- 1 teaspoon liquid smoke
- Half cup cider vinegar or white vinegar
- 1 tablespoon garlic powder
- 1 tablespoon onion powder
- 1 tablespoon chili powder
- 2 tablespoons dry mustard
- boiling water as needed

Per jar:

- 2 tablespoons brown or Muscavado sugar
- ½ onion

Directions:

1. Rinse and sort dried beans, then soak them in hot water for at least 2 hours.
2. Discard the soaking water, then bring to a boil in fresh water or broth.
3. Drain the beans again, this time reserving the cooking water.
4. Distribute the pork evenly across sanitized pint jars.
5. Top the meat with soaked beans, filling each jar no more than 2/3 full.
6. Bring tomato juice, vinegar, and spices to a boil.
7. Add to each jar a pinch of salt, brown sugar, and half an onion.
8. Ladle the hot tomato juice over the beans, leaving 1-1/2 inches of headspace. If necessary, top up with the bean cooking water. The beans must be totally covered with liquid and there must be room for them to expand.
9. Lid the jars and process in a pressure canner for 75 minutes for pints, 90 minutes for quarts, at 10 pounds of pressure, adjusting for altitude.

Boston Baked Beans

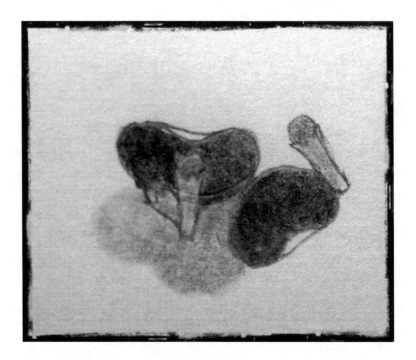

These beans are tangy and delicious right out of the jar. The liquid is the classic "Boston Baked Beans" sauce containing no tomato product. It thickens up beautifully during the canning process. We often add these beans to speed up a batch of homemade chili. The usual bean for this recipe is the navy bean, but I've also made it with pinto beans and the results were delicious.

Ingredients:

- 3 pounds dried beans
- 1 pound bacon or salt pork
- 6 tablespoons dark molasses
- 2 tablespoons white vinegar
- 2 tablespoons onion powder
- 1 tablespoon salt
- 2 teaspoon dry mustard
- ½ teaspoon powdered cloves

Directions:

1. Rinse and sort dried beans, then soak them in hot water for at least 2 hours.

2. Discard the soaking water, then bring to a boil in fresh water.
3. Drain the beans again, this time reserving the cooking water.
4. Distribute the bacon evenly across sanitized pint jars.
5. Top the bacon with soaked beans, filling each jar no more than 2/3 full.
6. In the bean pot, bring 6 cups of the reserved liquid (topping up with water to get to the 3 cups if necessary) to a boil. Stir in the rest of the ingredients, simmering until they are well combined.
7. Ladle the hot molasses mixture over the beans and bacon, leaving one inch of headspace.
8. Lid the jars and process in a pressure canner for 75 minutes for pints, 90 minutes for quarts, at 10 pounds of pressure, adjusting for altitude.

Hoppin' John

This classic black-eyed pea dish is a traditional New Year's Day meal in many parts of the world, said to bring the person who eats it on that day prosperity throughout the coming year.

Unlike the other recipes in this section, the black-eyed peas should NOT be soaked ahead of time.

Ingredients:

- 2 pounds chopped salt pork, bacon, or ham
- 3 pounds dried black-eyed peas
- 6 cloves garlic, smashed
- 2 cups diced green bell pepper
- 2 cups diced peeled fresh tomato
- 2 large onions, finely chopped
- Finely diced jalapeno pepper to taste (optional)
- Hot water as needed

Directions:

1. Layer the ingredients in 6 sanitized quart jars in the order listed, leaving 1 inch of headspace.
2. Pour hot water over the contents of the jars, allowing 1 inch of headspace for the peas to expand.
3. Use a utensil to slide around the edges of the jar to remove air pockets. Top up the liquid if necessary.
4. Lid the jars and process in a pressure canner for 90 minutes at 10 pounds of pressure, adjusting for altitude.

✦ Soups and Stews ✦

What could be nicer on a cold winter day than a piping hot bowl of soup?

Soup that came from a jar that you canned a couple of months previously!

When making soup, I recommend layering the ingredients. I don't always precook the soup with the ingredients all together because the flavors will meld beautifully during the pressure canning process.

The reason for layer is so that you get a somewhat equal amount of each item in your soup. Otherwise, you run the risk of having a jar of really chunky meaty soup and a jar that is mostly broth.

The other benefit is that this is a quick and easy method to prepare lots of delicious healthy meals!

Bestern Southwestern Chicken Soup

This Mexican-inspired soup is a family favorite. Be sure to soak the beans ahead of time for best result. There is no need to pre-cook them - they will cook nicely in the pressure canning process as long as they have been soaked.

Ingredients:

- 3 cups shredded cooked chicken
- 6 cups chicken broth
- 3 cans diced tomatoes (not drained)
- 3 cups black beans, rinsed, sorted, and pre-soaked
- 2 cans organic whole kernel corn or 2 cups of fresh or frozen corn kernels
- 1 onion, finely diced
- 4 cloves garlic, minced
- 1 bell pepper, diced
- 3 tablespoons chili powder
- 1 tablespoon cilantro
- 1 tablespoon cumin
- Salt and pepper

Directions:

1. In a large stock pot, stir together tomatoes, broth, chili powder, cilantro, cumin, salt, and pepper.
2. Bring this mixture to a boil.
3. Meanwhile layer the other ingredients evenly in your sanitized jars.
4. Top the layered ingredients with your hot broth mixture, leaving one inch of headspace. If you run out of broth, it's fine to top up your jars with water - the flavors will have plenty of time to blend
5. Lid your jars and process in a pressure canner for 90 minutes at 11 pounds of pressure. Be sure to adjust for altitude.

Serving suggestions:

Serve your delicious soup topped with a dollop of plain yogurt or sour cream and some crumbled tortilla chips. For heartier fare you can serve this over brown rice.

Splendiferous Split Pea Soup

On a crisp, cold winter day, what could be more deliciously comforting than some fresh crusty bread and a bowl of smoky split pea soup? This recipe is a household favorite and ideal for canning. When you heat it up, you may need to add some water or broth to get it to the consistency that you prefer. As is, you might be able to eat it with a fork!

This is a soup that can't be layered - you'll need to cook up a big pot of it for canning to get the right consistency.

Ingredients:

- 6 cups split peas, rinsed and sorted
- cups of water
- 1/2 pound of ham or bacon, diced (approx. 1 cup)
- 1 tablespoon olive oil
- 2 whole onions, finely chopped
- cloves of garlic, finely minced
- 3 carrots, peeled and cut into chunks
- 3-4 bay leaves
- 1 tablespoon thyme
- 1 teaspoon sage

Directions:

1. In a big Dutch oven or stock pot, sauté ham or bacon in olive oil until it is lightly browned.
2. Add in onions and garlic and sauté for about two more minutes. (You can prep these in the food processor)
3. Stir in all of the rest of the ingredients and bring to a boil.
4. Reduce heat and simmer, covered, for an hour to an hour and a half, until all ingredients are soft.
5. You can stop at this point if you like your pea soup a bit lumpier, but we prefer ours pureed to blend the flavors. If you are pureeing the soup, run it through the blender until it reaches the consistency you desire. Don't pulverize it – just make it a thick puree.
6. Fill quart jars and allow 1 inch of headspace.
7. Process in the pressure canner for 90 minutes at 12 pounds pressure, adjusting for altitude.

Serving suggestions:

Go crazy and sauté a little bacon or ham for the top of the soup. Drizzle with sour cream, and serve with fresh crusty bread for dipping.

Great Golumpki Soup

Isn't the word "Golumpki" simply fantastic? Golumpki is the Polish name for cabbage roll, a fantastically time consuming Eastern-European delicacy that I am way too lazy to make.

So, I turned it into soup, because soup is easy, particularly in this raw-pack recipe.

Ingredients:

- 3 pounds ground beef or ground pork
- salt and pepper as desired
- 6 cups shredded cabbage
- 1 and 1/2 cups shredded carrots
- 2 medium onions, finely chopped
- 6 cloves minced garlic
- 12 cups tomato juice.
- 1 and a half cups white vinegar
- 2 tablespoons oregano
- 2 tablespoons basil
- 3 tablespoons brown sugar

Directions:

1. Prep your shredded veggies and prepare to layer.
2. Divide your ingredients by the number of jars you'll be using - this makes 6 quarts of soup.
3. Proceed to layer the ingredients in equal parts in the following order: meat, cabbage, carrots, onion, and garlic.
4. In a large stockpot, combine tomato juice, sugar, vinegar, and herbs. Heat this mixture to a simmer.
5. Top the ingredients in the jars with your canning liquid.
6. If needed, top up with water, leaving an inch of headroom.
7. Process in a pressure canner at 11 pounds for 90 minutes. Be sure to adjust for altitude.

Serving suggestions:

It's great as is, right out of the jar. For a heartier meal you can add 1 cup of cooked rice, or to turn it into a casserole, cook 1 cup of rice into the liquid. Some people like it topped with a drizzle of sour cream.

Autumn Garden Stew

One great way to make use of all those tasty root veggies in your fall garden is with a hearty stew. Based on what you have available, you can mix and match the veggies below to your heart's content. Do not add flour or other thickener to your stew until you are ready to eat it. Thickeners do not store well when canned.

This is a raw-pack recipe – the meat and vegetables will cook in the pressure canner and do not need to be cooked ahead of time.

Ingredients:

- 4 pounds stew beef, cut into cubes
- 4-6 cups (total) cubed potatoes, parsnips, turnips and/or rutabaga (any ratio)
- 2 cups carrot rounds
- 3 cups finely chopped onion
- 6 cloves garlic, crushed and minced

Liquid:

- 8 cups water
- 1 tablespoon rubbed thyme
- ½ tablespoon marjoram
- 2 tablespoons parsley
- 2 MSG-free beef bouillon cubes (optional)

Directions:

1. In a stockpot, combine the ingredients for your liquid and bring to a boil.
2. Meanwhile, layer meat and vegetables into your sanitized jars in the order listed above.
3. Pour the hot liquid over the layered meat and vegetables.
4. Lid your jars and process them in your p-canner for 90 minutes at 10 pounds of pressure. Be sure to adjust for altitude.

Serving suggestion:

When you are ready to serve your stew, add 1 tablespoon of flour to half a cup of water and whisk into a paste. Stir this into your stew as you heat it up – this will make a thick, hearty gravy.

Chicken Needs Noodles Soup

If your family craves homemade chicken noodle soup when they are under the weather reach for this instead of the familiar red and white can. When you can your own soup, you know that you aren't feeding your family deadly neurotoxins in the form of MSG, which is present in nearly ALL conventional canned soups on the market.

This soup has everything but the noodles, and the reason for this is that noodles break down and turn into a goopy mess when they are canned. Some people will tell you that they have canned soup with noodles for years and that the noodles are perfect, but I have never had success. When it is soup time, simply pour it into a pot, bring it to a boil, and throw in the amount of pasta that you want.

You can make this with any kind of poultry.

Ingredients:

- 8 boneless skinless chicken thighs or 4 breasts
- 2 cups carrots, cut in circles
- 1 cup chopped celery
- 1 cup finely grated onion
- 8 cloves fresh garlic, mashed to release oils
- 4 bay leaves
- 1 tablespoon each of oregano, basil, thyme, and salt
- Water as needed

Directions:

1. In a stockpot, simmer chicken in water with your herbs and salt until it is fork tender and you can shred it (about 1 hour). Don't add your veggies yet!
2. Drain chicken, reserving cooking liquid. Discard the bay leaves.
3. Divide the chicken, celery, onion, and carrots evenly and layer the ingredients in your sanitized jars.
4. Pour your cooking liquid into the jars and then top them up with water until you have one inch of headspace remaining. You will look at this and say, wow, there is way more liquid than chicken and veggies – but that's important because you need additional liquid for serving time, when you cook the pasta in this.
5. Lid your jars and p-can at 11-12 pounds for 90 minutes, adjusting for altitude.

Serving suggestions:

If you're feeding someone with a tummy ailment, add a little bit of ginger to the soup when you are re-heating it. You can also add some fresh minced garlic at serving time. Add whatever grain works for you at the moment: pasta, rice, orzo, and barley are all delicious.

Why You Should Can Chili

Chili is the perfect meal for a snowy winter day. The recipes that follow provide two very different takes on the traditional chili and are both enormously popular at our house. They are assembled using the layering method and are raw-packed, making it simple to create up to family dinners at one cooking session. (Or more if you canner will hold it!) Another great thing about chili is the nutritional value: it's loaded with protein, vitamins, and fiber!

The canned chili that you get from the grocery store generally contains lower quality meats, the least expensive vegetables available, and relies on artificial flavors and chemicals like MSG for its taste. If you want a heat-and-eat meal, home canned chili makes a far better addition to your pantry.

Tips for Perfect Home-Canned Chili

Soak the beans ahead of time and they will cook perfectly during the canning process.

Feel free to take liberties with the ingredients, using whatever you are able to source healthfully. The seasoning is the important part! Raw pack all of the ingredients and load the jars using the layering method.

The chili will thicken as it sits on the shelf. You may need to thin it with a small amount of water or tomato juice at serving time.

Mexican-Texican Cowboy Chili

Ingredients:

- 2 pounds ground beef/ground turkey/ground whatever
- 1 cup diced onion
- 4 cloves minced garlic
- 2 cups dried pinto beans
- 1 cup diced bell pepper
- Jalapeno peppers as desired

Liquid:

- 8 cups crushed tomatoes/tomato juice
- 1 can of beer (or water if you don't have beer on hand)
- ½ cup chili powder
- 1 tablespoon cumin
- 1 tablespoon salt
- 1 tablespoon parsley
- Water as needed

Directions:

1. In a stockpot, bring all liquid ingredients except for water to a boil.
2. Meanwhile, layer your meat, dried beans, onions, garlic, and bell pepper evenly across your sanitized jars – this will make 4 quarts of very thick chili.
3. Pour your hot liquid mixture over the layered ingredients, then top off with water, leaving an inch of headspace.
4. Process at 10 pounds of pressure for an hour and a half in your p-canner. Be sure to adjust for altitude.

Sweet & Spicy Chili

This recipe is awesome if you happen to acquire some venison or other game. A lot of people are uncomfortable with the unfamiliar "wild" flavor of the meat and this extremely well-seasoned chili hides that. Minus the jalapenos (at least in my world!) this is a very kid-friendly flavor.

Ingredients:

- 4-6 pounds stewing beef/stewing whatever
- 1 slice bacon per jar
- 2 large onion, diced
- 6 cloves garlic, minced
- 1 tablespoon sea salt
- 3 cups dried red kidney beans
- 1 cup bell pepper, diced
- Finely minced jalapeno pepper to taste

Liquid:

- 8 cups tomato puree
- ½ cup apple cider vinegar
- ½ cup brown sugar or molasses
- ½ cup chili powder
- 1 teaspoon dry mustard
- Water as needed

Directions:

1. In a stockpot, bring all liquid ingredients except for water to a boil.
2. Layer your raw meat, dried beans, bacon, onions, garlic, and bell pepper evenly across your prepped jars – this will make 4 quarts of very thick chili.
3. Pour your hot liquid mixture over the layered ingredients, then top off with water as needed, leaving an inch of headspace.
4. Process at 10 pounds of pressure for an hour and a half in your p-canner. Be sure to adjust for altitude.
5. When serving your chili, be sure to shred the bacon with a fork and stir it in.

❧ Canning Your Own Recipes ❦

Canning recipes are great to have, but they aren't absolutely necessary. Now, the USDA might disagree, but I firmly believe that if you have a grasp on food safety principals and canning basics, that you can preserve your own recipes.

You need to follow the basics rules of canning. When canning your own recipes, search for instructions on how to can the separate ingredients. Calculate the processing time by using the time for the ingredient that requires the *longest* time to be preserved safely.

So, for example, if you're canning a roast with carrots, onions and beef, the carrots require 20 minutes, the onions require 30 minutes and the beef requires 90 minutes. Thus, 90 minutes of pressure canning is required to safely can this recipe.

You should also note whether or not the individual ingredients have special requirements when they are canned. Always use the longest time and the most stringent requirements to make sure your food is safe.

The USDA Complete Guide to Home Canning has a lot of great information on safely canning many different separate ingredients. (And it's a free download!)

I have to stress that the onus for your family's safety is upon you. Because I cannot predict every single ingredient of every single recipe a person might wish to can, I can't give you a comprehensive list of dos and don'ts.

If there is any doubt as to the safety of something you intend to can, don't do it.

can tell you that the USDA does NOT recommend canning the following:

- Dairy Products
- Flour and other thickeners
- Grains like pasta or rice (they wouldn't hold up to the canning process anyway)

As I mentioned above, you need to check the ingredients you intend to include in your recipe against the USDA guidelines. Botulism is no laughing matter - it can kill or paralyze you. I believe that you possess the good judgment and ability to look up your separate ingredients and omit them if they should not be canned. It's not worth risking the health of your family.

Some recipes will do very well canned, some need a tweak, and others simply won't work at all.

If you recipe calls for grains, like pasta or rice, omit them during the canning process and add them at serving time.

Some ingredients have flavors that "turn" when you can them. Sage, for example, tastes terrible when canned. I've always used it as an ingredient in my chicken soup, so I didn't think twice about adding the herb to some soup that I canned. When I opened and heated up the soup, it was absolutely foul! I had no idea what it was initially but upon researching it, I learned that sage has a propensity for "turning." Spinach as an ingredient, I have also learned from unpleasant experience, gives a terrible flavor to the entire dish.

While we're talking about flavors, keep in mind that the spices and seasonings that you use will intensify as the jar sits there in your cupboard. For some foods, this is a great bonus - like spaghetti sauce! For others, it can be overwhelming. If you heat something up, like a soup or stew, and find the flavor is overpowering, often you can rectify it by adding a few cups of broth. Ham in particular gets incredibly strong. I only use ham that I have canned as an ingredient in something else - it works well in a pot of beans or in scalloped potatoes.

Just because it looks unpleasant in the jar doesn't necessarily mean tha it's bad. Meat often looks rather unappetizing in the jar - the fat separates and floats to the top or the sides of the jar. Simply stir it back in or dispose of it. Split pea soup also looks absolutely dreadful.

Fat brings me to another tip - it can be risky to can foods that are extremely high in fat - they become rancid far more easily than leaner meats.

If your recipe calls for the addition of flour or sour cream as a thickener, omit those ingredients during the canning process. It is far tastier (and safer) to add those ingredients during the reheating process. When I make beef stew, for example, I can the stew ingredients and herbs in a broth or water, then when reheating, I dip out a small ladle-full of liquid and stir in flour to make a hearty gravy.

Once you have the hang of canning using recipes, it's really simple to modify your own recipes.

Happy canning!

❧ Appendices ❧

Fruit Canning Chart

Fruit is high acid and may be canned in a water bath canner.
You may can fruit in a heavy syrup, a light syrup, a non-overpowering
fruit juice like apple or white grape, or water.

FRUIT	SPECIAL INSTRUCTIONS	PROCESSING TIME
Apricot	Peel, slice in half to pit	5 minutes
Blackberry	optional step: mill to remove seeds	10 minutes
Blueberry	optional step: puree	7 minutes
Cherry	Pit with a cherry pitter, chop before cooking	10 minutes
Grape	Mill to remove seeds	10 minutes
Huckleberry	Check for stems	10 minutes
Peach	Peel, slice in half to remove pits	10 minutes
Plum	Slice in half to remove pits	5 minutes
Raspberry	Crush with a potato masher	10 minutes
Strawberry	Remove cores, mash with a potato masher	10 minutes

Vegetable Canning Chart

Vegetables are a low-acid food and must be processed in a pressure canner, with a baseline of 11 pounds of pressure, and adjustments for altitude.

Food	Time for Pints	Time for Quarts
Asparagus	30	40
Beans (green or yellow)	20	25
Beets	30	35
Carrots	25	30
Corn	55	85
Lima Beans	40	50
Okra	25	40
Peas (Field)	40	40
Peppers	35	
Potatoes (white)	35	40
Potatoes (sweet)	65	90
Pumpkin	55	90
Squash (winter)	55	90

I Say To-may-to, You Say To-mah-to

It's tomato season, or, as I like to call it, "Make Your Kitchen Look like a Crime Scene" season!

I'm not gonna lie – there is nothing messier than a bushel of tomatoes getting turned into jars of tomato loveliness. It's a fair bit of work to process your own tomato products, but the intensely flavored results make it all worthwhile.

These are some short-cuts to speed along your tomato processing procedures.

Peeling the Tomatoes:

Lots of people already know this little trick but it bears repeating, especially when you are looking at an entire bushel of those bad boys!

1. Begin boiling a pot of water on the stove.
2. Also prep a large receiving bowl with very icy ice water.
3. Slide tomatoes into a pot of boiling water for 1-2 minutes – you will know they are ready to come out because the skin will start to wrinkle up a little bit.
4. Use a slotted spoon to remove the tomatoes and drop them instantly into the ice bath, where you can leave them for as long as you need to.
5. Once the tomato is cool enough to touch, you can easily use your fingers to slide the skin off.

(***FYI Bonus*** This process also works like a charm on thin-skinned fruits like peaches, nectarines and apricots.)

Coring the Tomatoes

There's more than one way to skin a cat – er, core a tomato!
- You can simply use a paring knife and cut it out.
- You can use an old-fashioned hand crank food mill that spits the bad stuff out one end and the good stuff out the other end.

Now your tomatoes are prepped and ready for whatever you feel like creating!

Turning Tomatoes into a Sauce-Like Consistency

Turning your tomatoes into a sauce-like consistency can be done in three different ways.

1. You can dump the whole mess of cored and peeled tomatoes into a big stock pot, just as they are, or roughly chopped, and cook them down.
2. You can puree them by batches in a food processor or blender and then cook them down.
3. You can put them through the above mentioned food mill, then into the stock pot, and cook them down.

For me, the choice relies on what I am making. For spaghetti sauces, I prefer the consistency of the tomatoes that come out of the food mill.
If I'm making sauces, like ketchup or barbecue sauce, I prefer to use the food processor.

Consider your tomatoes officially prepped – from this point on you are ready to proceed with your recipe!

Removing Pesticide from Produce

While I would love for every bite we consume to be organic, budgetary restrictions don't always allow for it. Furthermore, even USDA-certified organic produce sometimes has an application of antibiotics, particularly orchard fruits.

What's more, because of chemtrails and spraying of nearby farms, even organic veggies can have some toxins. I use this process for cleaning all of our food before consuming or preserving it.

It helps to purchase produce from local farms and have a good relationship with a couple of favorite fellows in overalls. This way, you can quiz them about what is sprayed on the goodies before you bring them home.

One important fact that many people don't realize is the high price of becoming "certified organic" - it is literally tens of thousands of dollars. This being the case, a lot of local produce is organic, just not certified organic.

So what can we do about those fruits and veggies that get sprayed? Apples, for example, can have more than 48 different pesticides on them, according to a report by the Environmental Working Group. You can clean off more than 95% of the pesticides if you are diligent in your process.

1. Put 1 cup of baking soda and some all natural dish soap into a sink full of hot water. For more delicate produce like berries or lettuce, use cool water.

2. Allow your produce to soak in the solution for about 20 minutes. An alarming white film of gunk may rise to the top of the sink.

3. Drain the sink and rinse the produce. For hardy produce you can rinse it under running water. For delicate produce, scrub your sink clean, fill it with fresh water, and swish the produce around in the clean water to rinse it.

4. For thick-skinned firm produce, use a cloth and scrub the outside of the item. For more delicate produce, allow it to drain in a colander.

5. If you are still able to see a film or if the rinse water is cloudy, clean out your sink with white vinegar and repeat the process.

Acknowledgements:

This project absolutely would not have been possible without unflagging support from my friends in the industry, Mac Slavo of SHTFplan, Ed Thomas and Lily Dane of The Daily Sheeple, Tess Pennington of Ready Nutrition, and Lizzie Bennett of Underground Medic.

I'd like to thank my exceptionally patient and tolerant daughters, for your forbearance in trying the food experiments and going on all of the "adventures" and loving me regardless of your rather unconventional upbringing. R, you are following in the family tradition and are an incredibly talented writer – you blow me away – and you are a kind, beautiful soul, inside and out. C, your charming illustrations add so much to this book, and I am so incredibly proud of the amazing, sweet, and talented adult you have become. You are both wonderful, creative, caring, self-sufficient girls. You two are the shining lights of my life. I would not be at this place in life without your love and support. I love you.

Thank you also to my dearest friends who shall remain nameless in order to protect their privacy - you are priceless.

And finally thank you to my mom and dad, for the great start in life you gave to me. Mom, thanks for pushing me, even though I didn't appreciate it much at the time. Daddy - you are missed every day and your calm, patient intelligence will always be my greatest inspiration.

About Daisy

Daisy Luther is the author of *The Pantry Primer: How to Build a One Year Food Supply in Three Month*s. She lives with her family and assorted animals in a small village in the Pacific Northwestern area of the United States. On her website, The Organic Prepper, Daisy writes about healthy prepping, homesteading adventures, and the pursuit of liberty and food freedom. You can reach her by email at daisy@theorganicprepper.ca

About C. Morgan

C. Morgan is a freelance photographer and illustrator. She attends college in Ontario, Canada. *The Organic Canner* is the first book in which her charming illustrations have appeared. She can be reached in care of the author at the above email address.

51001610R00136

Made in the USA
Lexington, KY
09 April 2016